lynne Cope

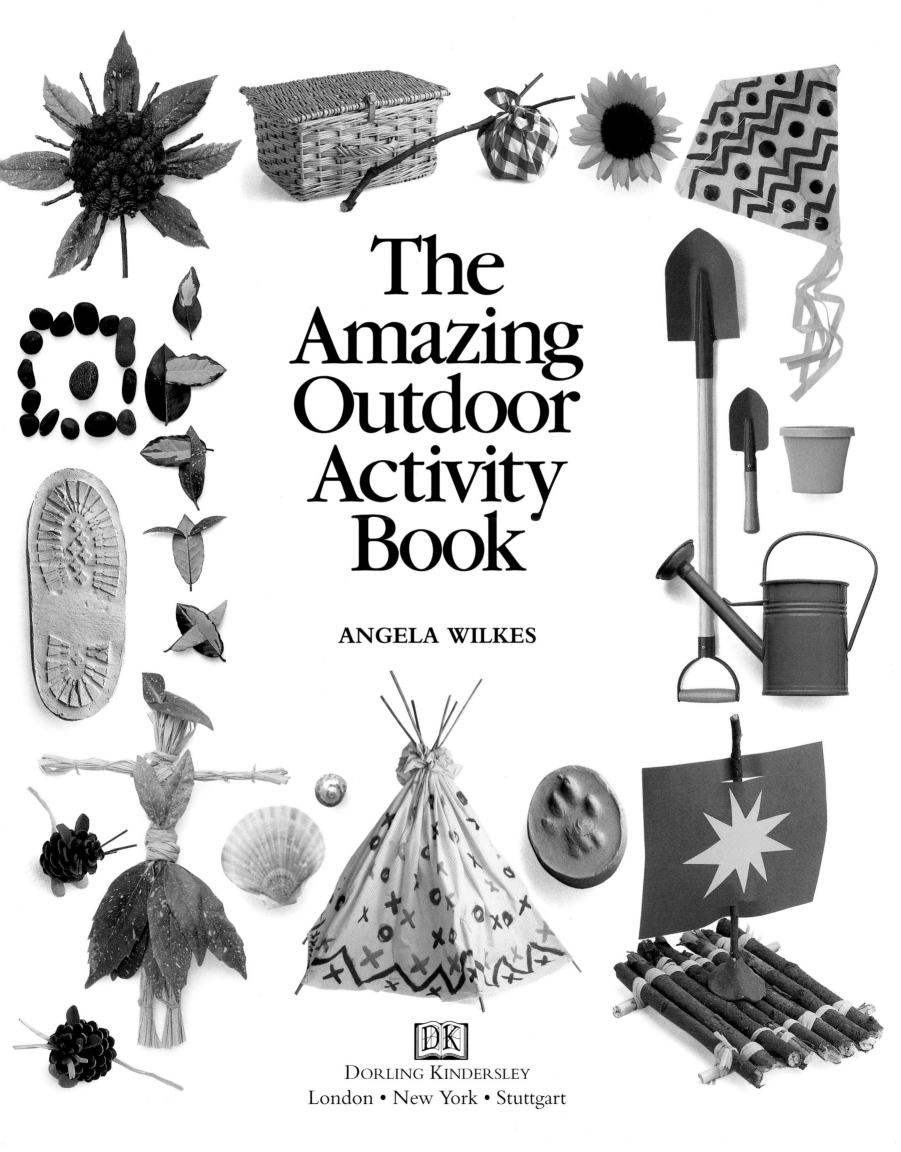

The Amazing Outdoor Activity Book

ANGELA WILKES

DK

DORLING KINDERSLEY
London • New York • Stuttgart

DK

A Dorling Kindersley Book

*For Heather and But, in memory
of all our childhood expeditions.*

Designer Jane Bull
Photographer Dave King

Project Editor Stella Love
Managing Editor Jane Yorke
Senior Art Editor Chris Scollen
Production Josie Alabaster

First published in Great Britain in 1996
by Dorling Kindersley Limited
9 Henrietta Street, London WC2E 8PS

A CIP catalogue record for this book
is available from the British Library.

ISBN 0-7513-5372-8

Colour reproduction by Colourscan, Singapore
Printed and bound in Italy by A. Mondadori Editore, Verona

Dorling Kindersley would like to thank Mandy Earey for invaluable
design assistance, Chris Branfield for jacket design, Joanne Downey for
text fitting, Helen Drew and Carey Combe for editorial help, Cathy Mann
for food preparation, and Stephen Bull. Dorling Kindersley would also like
to thank the following models for appearing in this book: Holly Cowgill,
Kelly Gomeze, Emma Judson, Lawrence King, Jade Ogugua,
Sam Priddy, Tebergé Ricketts, Tim Shaw, and Darren Singh.
The project models were made by Jane Bull and Angela Wilkes.

CONTENTS

INTRODUCTION

This book is full of great ideas for things to do and make outdoors all year round. As well as being fun, many of the projects will help you to find out all kinds of fascinating things about the natural world. Read through the activities and decide which one to try, then start collecting useful materials. When you finish a project, remember to put away all your equipment, and to clean up any mess.

Equipment and materials to collect

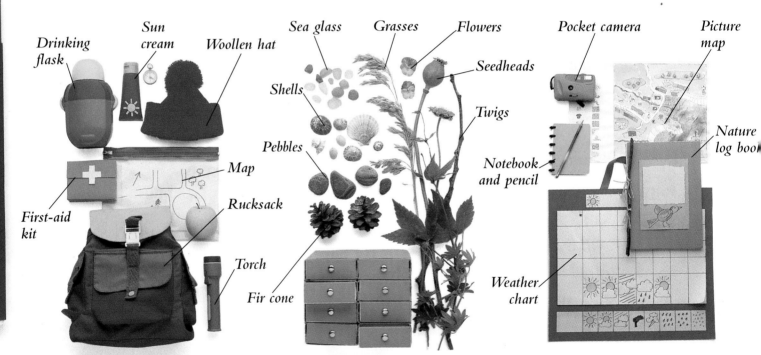

Drinking flask

Sun cream

Woollen hat

First-aid kit

Map

Rucksack

Torch

Fir cone

Sea glass

Grasses

Flowers

Seedheads

Shells

Pebbles

Twigs

Pocket camera

Picture map

Notebook and pencil

Nature log book

Weather chart

Outdoor living
It is important to be properly equipped on expeditions and trips. These are some of the items you should take along with you.

Nature collections
Collecting interesting things you find outdoors is a good starting point for learning about nature. This book gives you ideas on what to collect and how to display it.

Keeping records
You can learn a lot by recording your observations. Find out how to draw maps, keep a log book, and make your own weather chart.

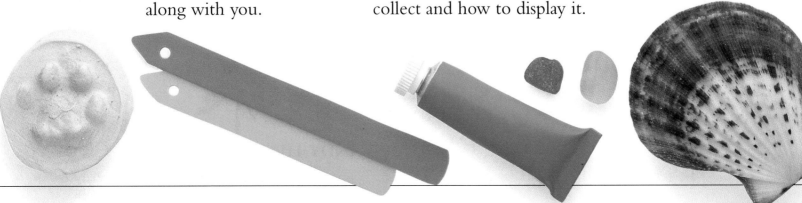

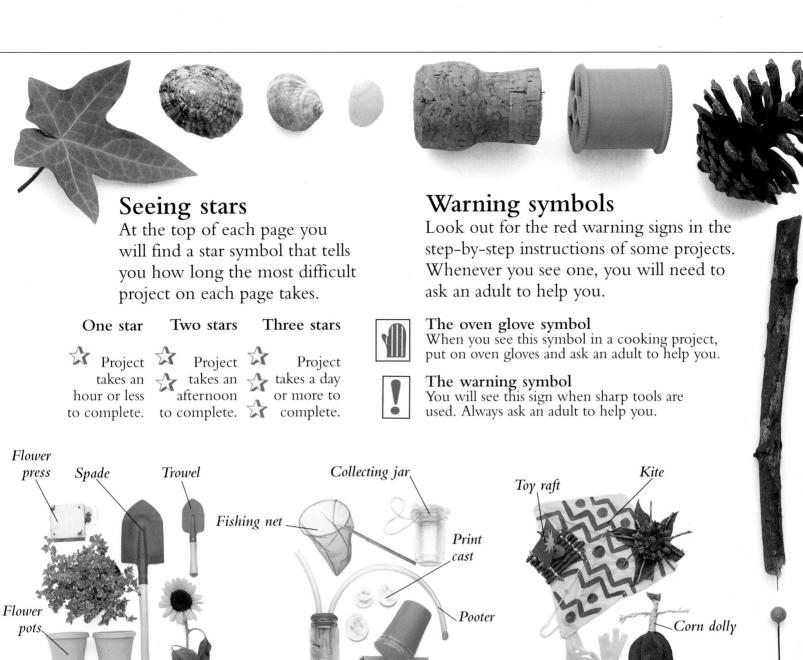

Seeing stars

At the top of each page you will find a star symbol that tells you how long the most difficult project on each page takes.

One star	Two stars	Three stars
☆ Project takes an hour or less to complete.	☆☆ Project takes an afternoon to complete.	☆☆☆ Project takes a day or more to complete.

Warning symbols

Look out for the red warning signs in the step-by-step instructions of some projects. Whenever you see one, you will need to ask an adult to help you.

The oven glove symbol
When you see this symbol in a cooking project, put on oven gloves and ask an adult to help you.

The warning symbol
You will see this sign when sharp tools are used. Always ask an adult to help you.

Flower press *Spade* *Trowel*

Flower pots

Watering can

Collecting jar

Fishing net

Print cast

Pooter

Binoculars

Toy raft *Kite*

Corn dolly

Driftwood seagull

Fir cone mice

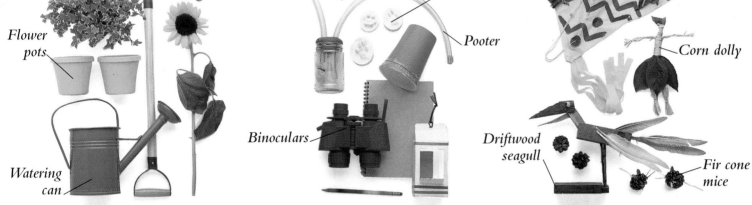

Plant power

The best way to find out about plants is to grow them. Start your own garden from scratch, grow huge plants from tiny seeds, and press your own flowers.

Animal watch

From catching your own minibeasts to taking casts of animal footprints, there are plenty of ideas on how to attract and then watch wildlife.

Toys and models

You can have great fun outdoors by making your own toys such as a kite, or a toy boat. Or try turning natural materials into unusual models.

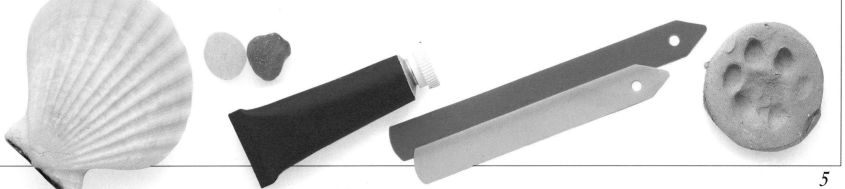

OUTDOOR SURVIVAL KIT

Exploring the great outdoors is exciting, but it is important that you are properly kitted before you go. Wear comfortable clothes and shoes and pack everything else you need, such as food, maps, and a waterproof anorak, in a rucksack. Here are all the essential items you will need, together with ideas for things you might find useful for some nature detective work.

Being prepared

Plan your route before you go, and listen to the weather forecast in the morning so that you know what to wear and what to take with you.

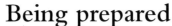

Peaked cap

Headgear

A woolly hat will keep your head warm in cold weather. When it is hot, a peaked cap will keep the sun out of your eyes.

Woolly hat

Pocket compass

Waterproof anorak

Finding the way

Take a map and a compass to help you find your way. Be sure to let your parents know where you are going and how long you expect to be out.

Rucksack

The best rucksacks have lots of useful pockets.

Money belt

A money belt is useful for keeping coins and small items handy.

Maps and plastic wallet

A plastic wallet will keep your maps dry.

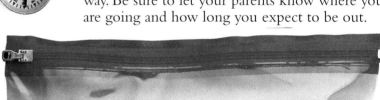

What to take

Here are some suggestions for things to carry. Some are essential, such as food and drink, some will help you in case of an accident, and others will help you to study things that you see.

Sweets and chocolate will give you energy.

First-aid kit

Rations and supplies
If you are going out for longer than half a day, you will need food and drink to keep you going.

Take some water or juice to drink.

Plastic lunch box

Flask

Other essentials
A first-aid kit, tissues, money, a torch, and sun cream are all important extras to take with you.

Protect your skin on sunny days.

Tissues

Carry coins and useful phone numbers in a small purse in case you need to phone for help.

Sun cream

Torch

Purse

Nature spotting
When you are out walking, you may want to make notes and sketches of insects, flowers, and birds, or collect interesting finds. The items shown here will help you.

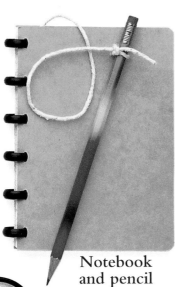

Take a small camera with you in case you see anything unusual.

Camera

Notebook and pencil

Pair of binoculars

Plastic bags and containers

Bug bottle

Pocket magnifying glass

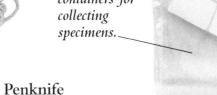

Length of string

Carry some containers for collecting specimens.

Penknife

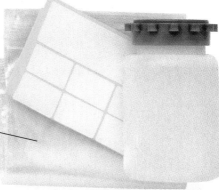

UNDER COVER

Being able to build a simple shelter is a useful survival skill, but it can also be great fun to do in your own garden. You can make a wigwam from canes and a large piece of material. It is easier to make if you have a friend with you. Or why not make a portable hide so you can watch animals and birds in close-up without them seeing you? Turn the page to see the finished wigwam and hide.

EQUIPMENT

Ruler

Scissors

5 cm paintbrush

Felt pen

Jars of water

You will need

For the hide

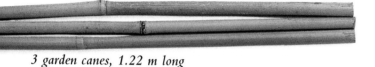

3 garden canes, 1.22 m long

A piece of calico or old sheet,
5 m by 1.5 m

A piece of calico or sheeting, 1.35 m by 96 cm

String

For the wigwam

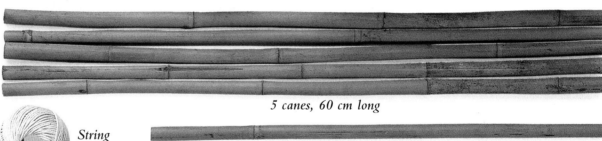

5 canes, 60 cm long

String

1 cane, 45 cm long

Making the wigwam

Large, strong elastic bands

Large pots of poster paint or fabric paint

6 garden canes, 2 m long

1 Stand the six garden canes together so that the tops meet. Tie strong elastic bands around them 38 cm from the top to make a frame.

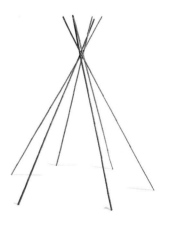

2 Ask a friend to hold the standing canes steady at the top and splay them out until they are about 84 cm apart at the bottom, as shown.

3 Use a length of string to tie each of the five 60 cm canes to a long cane so they cross. Wind the string around the canes and tie a reef knot★.

4 Position the five 60 cm canes about 63 cm up from the bottom of each of the long, standing canes, as shown. Leave a space for an opening.

5 Tie the 45 cm cane across the last two long canes about 85 cm down from the elastic bands, to make the door frame of the wigwam.

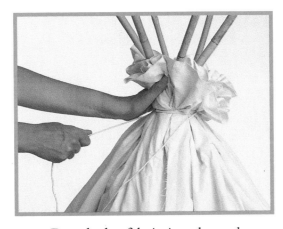

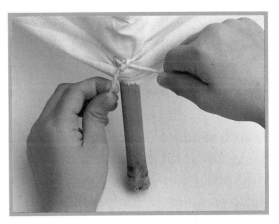

6 Ask a friend to hold the fabric half over the door of the wigwam. Wrap the fabric around the canes, so the two ends meet at the door.

7 Bunch the fabric in where the canes are tied together at the top. Wind a piece of string tightly around the fabric and tie a reef knot.

8 Pull the fabric down each cane. Tie it at the bottom by cutting two holes in the fabric, tying the string through them, and around the canes.

9 Tie the fabric to the canes in the same way where the shorter canes are tied to the long canes and at the top of each side of the door.

10 Mix paint and water in jars and use a large paintbrush to paint the wigwam fabric with bold shapes, such as circles and crosses.

11 Paint a decorative border along the bottom and around the door opening to complete the wigwam design.

★ See page 62.

SIMPLE SHELTERS

Making the hide

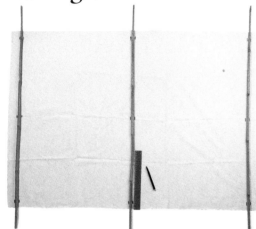

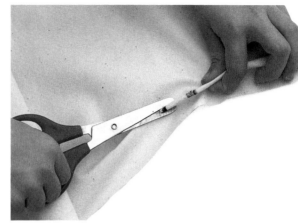

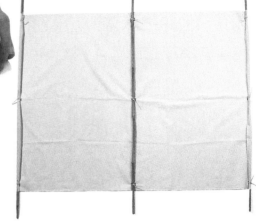

1 Spread out fabric for the hide flat on the ground. Lay the three canes across it as shown, with one at each end and one in the middle.

2 With a pen, make marks on both sides of each cane near the top, the bottom, and in the centre. Then cut a small hole on each mark.

3 Thread a piece of string through each set of holes and round the cane between them. Then knot the strings to fix the fabric to the canes.

Invisible observers

From behind your hide you can watch wildlife close up. Take a rug to sit on and have your binoculars and notepad handy. Remember to keep as quiet as you possibly can.

Heading home
To take the hide home, pull it out of the ground, fold it in half along the centre cane and roll it up.

Make sure the slits are big enough for your binoculars.

Setting up
To set up the hide, stretch it out to its full width and push each cane into the ground. If the ground is hard, ask an adult to help you. The hide is big enough to conceal two people. You can paint your hide green and brown to camouflage it.

Closed wigwam

When the door of the wigwam is closed, the two ends of the fabric should meet halfway across the opening. The wigwam is not waterproof, so remember to put it away at night, or if it rains.

4 Draw two letter-box slits on the fabric halfway between the centre and each outer cane and 25 cm down from the top edge. Cut out the slits.

You can copy these decorations for your wigwam or try out ideas of your own.

Setting up camp

Choose a flat, dry place to set up your wigwam and then splay out the canes until the fabric is fairly taut. Put a waterproof rug inside to make it cosy, and stock it with the supplies you need.

Fold the fabric flaps back around the door canes when you want the door open.

RATIONS AND SUPPLIES

Whether you are going on a day's hike, a secret expedition, or just into the park, you will get hungry and need rations to keep you going. What food you take will be limited by how you are going to carry it, but every picnic has the same basic elements. Include something savoury, something sweet, a drink, and treats to nibble.

Savoury fillers

Make a roll or sandwich the main part of your rations and fill it with your favourite things. Try not to overfill it so that it is easy to eat, and wrap it in foil or clingfilm to keep it fresh.

Tuna, mayonnaise, and cucumber roll

Roll filled with salami, sliced cheese, and salad

Pitta bread stuffed with salami, sliced cucumber, and tomato

Small French stick filled with sliced ham and salad

Sweet things

Biscuits and small pieces of cake are good for picnics and do not take up much room in your bag. Take more than you think you need and add some pieces of fresh fruit.

Chocolate brownies

Shortbread biscuits

Apple

Bunches of grapes

Pear

Clementine

Savoury extras

If you are going on a special picnic, you could take along salad or vegetable sticks in small containers, and small individually wrapped cheeses.

Sticks of pepper, cucumber, and carrot

Thirst quenchers

Take as much drink as you can carry. Water and fruit juice are more refreshing than fizzy drinks. In cold weather you could take a hot drink or soup in a flask. Make sure you screw on the lids of drinks tightly.

Water bottle filled with fruit juice

Different small cheeses

Small vacuum flask for cold or hot drinks, or soup

Quick snacks and nibbles

It is a good idea to pack a few snacks and quick treats. Put them in one of the pockets of your rucksack. Remember to take the wrappers home with you.

Crisps

Nuts and raisins

Sweets

Mini chocolate bars

Packing your rations

If you are going on a hike, you will need to pack your food in a small lunch box and put it in your rucksack. For a picnic you could use a picnic basket or cool bag. Why not make your own carrier for a picnic in the park or garden?

Small picnic basket

Traveller's bundle on a stick

OUTDOOR FEAST

What simpler way to cook than to wrap your food in foil and bake it in your camp fire. Use thick baking foil to wrap the food, folding in the edges tightly. Wait until the flames die down, then ask an adult to help you push the parcels into the glowing embers. Here you can find out how to bake potato surprise, apples, and garlic and herb bread in foil. These recipes make one portion.

EQUIPMENT

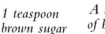

Sharp knife

Apple corer

Teaspoon

Chopping board

Cheese grater

Baking foil

Small bowl

You will need

For the potato surprise

1 large potato

Ham cut in cubes

1 chopped tomato

Grated cheese

For the baked apple

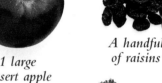

1 large dessert apple

A handful of raisins

1 teaspoon brown sugar

A knob of butter

For the garlic and herb bread

1 small French stick

55 g cream cheese

Chives

Parsley

1/4 teaspoon salt

1 clove of garlic

Potato surprise

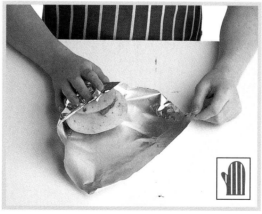

1 Slice a lid off the potato and scoop out the inside with the apple corer. Fill the hollow with chopped ham, tomato, and the cheese.

2 Put the lid back on the potato and wrap it in baking foil. Bake it for 1 to 1½ hours until it is soft in the centre and cooked right through.

Garlic and herb bread

1 Chop the parsley, chives, and garlic. Mix the salt and herbs into the cream cheese and beat it with a spoon until the mixture is soft.

2 Make cuts along the bread and spread the cheese mix inside them. Wrap the foil around the bread and bake it for 15 minutes.

Baked apple

1 Lay the apple on two overlapping squares of baking foil. Core the apple and fill the hole with raisins. Spoon some brown sugar on top.

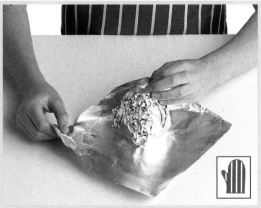

2 Put the knob of butter on top of the sugar and wrap the apple in both layers of foil. Then bake it for 30 to 40 minutes, until it is soft.

An outdoor feast

Ask an adult to take the foil parcels out of the fire for you. Let the parcels cool a little and then unwrap them. Test the potato and apple with a sharp knife to make sure they are soft. If not, wrap them up again and put them back in the embers to cook for longer.

Potato surprise

Serve the foil parcels in paper napkins so that people do not burn their fingers.

When eating outside, use plastic spoons to eat your potato and apple.

Baked apple

Use two layers of foil for baked apples to protect the apple skin from burning.

Garlic and herb bread

FIRESIDE COOKING

Food grilled outdoors on a barbecue has a special smoky flavour all of its own. Even the simplest things taste delicious. Here you can find out how to barbecue sausage kebabs and beefburgers. Prepare the food indoors, then take it out to the barbecue to be cooked. Make sure there is an adult there to help you. The recipes here will serve four people.

EQUIPMENT

Fork

Sharp knife

Mixing bowl

Fish slice

4 skewers

Chopping board

You will need

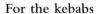

For the kebabs

1 red onion

1 courgette

1 red and 1 green pepper

450 g small sausages

Cherry tomatoes

For the beefburgers

450 g minced beef

4 sesame seed buns

1 egg yolk

1/2 an onion, finely chopped

Salt and pepper

For garnishing

Sliced cheese

Sliced tomato

Sliced cucumber

Lettuce

Making the kebabs

1 Remove the cores and pith out of the peppers and cut them into squares. Slice the courgette in rounds, and cut the peeled onion into quarters.

2 Thread the chopped vegetables and sausages on to the skewers as shown. Be very careful with the sharp points on the skewers.

3 Ask an adult to check when the barbecue is ready. Then grill the kebabs for 10 to 15 minutes, turning them so that they cook all over.

Making the beefburgers

1 Put the minced beef, egg yolk, finely chopped onion, and salt and pepper into the mixing bowl. Mix them together well with one hand.

2 Split the mixture into four even-sized parts. Roll each one into a ball, then flatten it and firm round the edges to make a circular beefburger.

3 When the barbecue is hot, put the beefburgers on the grill and cook them for 5 to 10 minutes on each side, until they are firm and brown.

The open-air grill

You can eat the kebabs straight away. Pick up the skewers carefully as they will be hot, then slide the sausages and vegetables off on to your plate, using a fork. Assemble the beefburgers as shown below, for a real feast!

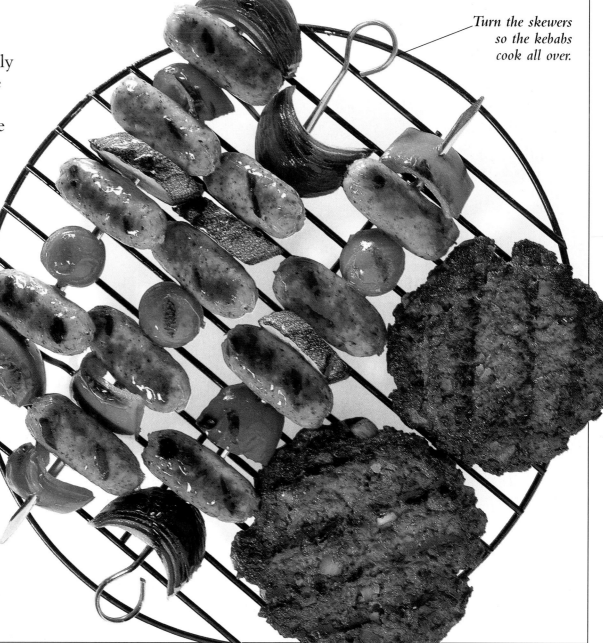

Turn the skewers so the kebabs cook all over.

All in a bun
Arrange each beefburger in a bun with a slice of cheese, sliced tomato, cucumber, and some crisp lettuce.

Other kebabs
You can vary your kebabs by using cubes of chicken or lamb, or adding small mushrooms.

ANIMAL TRACKS

You can keep a permanent record of animal prints you come across outside by making casts of them from plaster of Paris. If you can't find clear animal prints why not start by making casts of hand and footprints you have made yourself. It is great fun and produces clear casts for your nature museum.

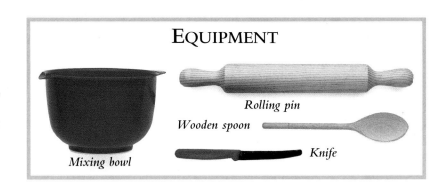

EQUIPMENT

Rolling pin

Wooden spoon

Knife

Mixing bowl

You will need

(For one large plaster cast)

Strips of card

Clingfilm

300 ml water

Paper clips

Self-hardening modelling clay if you are making your own prints★

420 g plaster of Paris★

Making a print

1 Lay clingfilm on your work top. Cut a lump of clay off the block and place it on the clingfilm, then roll it out until it is about 1 cm thick.

2 Press your hand, foot, or shoe firmly down onto the clay to make a clear print, then lift it off again without wriggling.

Making a cast

1 Bend a strip of card into a circle big enough to go around the print. Clip the ends together and push it into the clay around the print.

★*Available from good toy shops, or art supply shops.*

2 Put the plaster of Paris in the mixing bowl and pour in the water. Mix them with your wooden spoon, until smooth and runny.

3 Gently pour the plaster mixture into the card ring until it is about 2.5 cm deep. Leave it for around 15 minutes until the plaster has set hard.

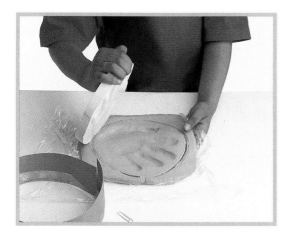

4 Unclip the card and peel it off the plaster. Gently ease the fragile plaster cast away from the clay mould. Leave the cast to set for a day.

Animal casts

You can take casts of animal tracks outdoors in the same way. Simply push a card ring into the mud or sand around each print, and then follow the instructions for making a cast.

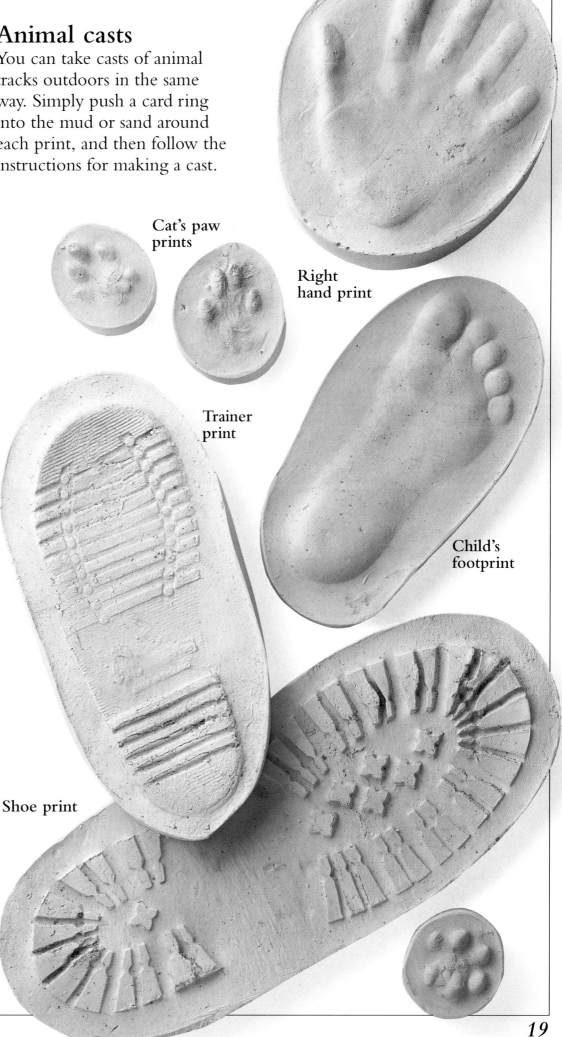

Cat's paw prints

Right hand print

Trainer print

Child's footprint

Shoe print

ON THE TRAIL

Tracking skills can be really useful for finding your way about. Here you can find out how to lay and follow a trail using different materials. Choose things that will show up on the ground and collect enough of them for the whole trail. Then you can have fun with your friends laying a simple trail, or inventing one with coded signs to follow.

A trail code

You will need a friend to lay a trail for you to follow. If you use a coded trail, you must both agree what the signs mean and keep a record of them in your notebook. Here are some useful signs made with sticks, stones, and leaves.

You will need

(Any one of the following things)

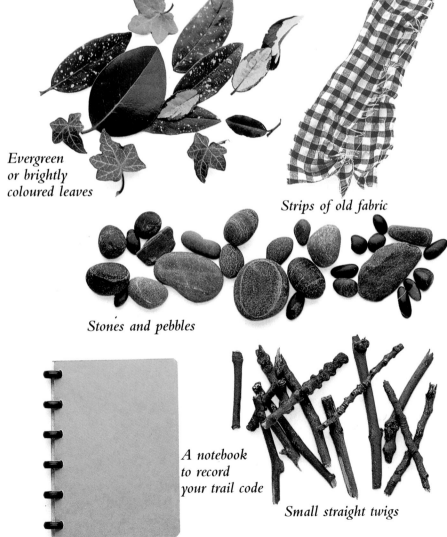

Evergreen or brightly coloured leaves

Strips of old fabric

Stones and pebbles

A notebook to record your trail code

Small straight twigs

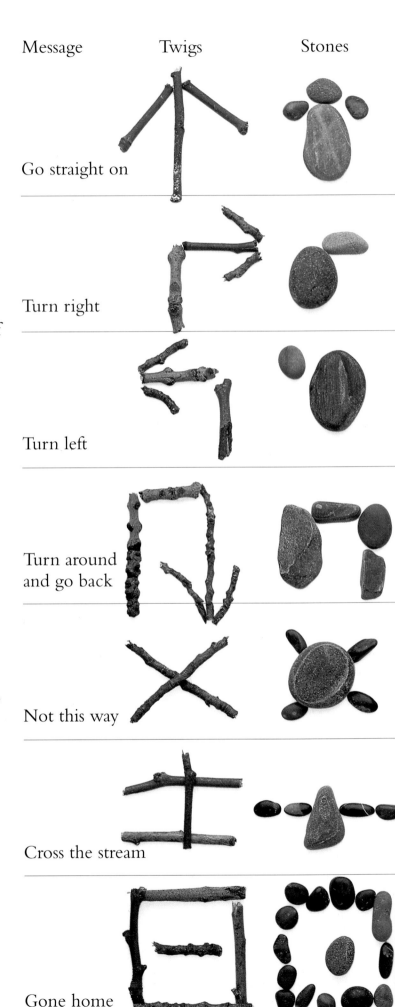

Message	Twigs	Stones
Go straight on		
Turn right		
Turn left		
Turn around and go back		
Not this way		
Cross the stream		
Gone home		

Leaves

Plain trails
You do not have to lay a coded trail. You could make simple direction arrows on the ground with leaves, twigs, or stones.

Tell-tale signs
You could tie strips of fabric to bushes or low-lying branches to show which way to go. Remember to remove them all and take them home afterwards.

Direction arrow made from pebbles

Trail game

Why not play a trail game? You will need at least two people to lay and follow a trail, but it is more fun if there are four of you so that you can work together in pairs. Two of you lay the trail and the other two have to see if they can follow it all the way to the end.

Before you start, work out the trail code together so that you all know what the signs mean. Give the trail layers a ten minute headstart or, if the trail is going to be around a garden, let them finish laying it before the followers set off. And no peeping!

Laying the trail
Always lay the signs on the same side of the path, and put them where they show up. Space them about five metres apart so that the followers do not have too far to go between each one.

Make sure you lay the signs very clearly at any tricky spots, such as where a path forks, or where the grass grows long.

Direction arrow made from leaves

MAKING A MAP

Being able to find your way about is a vital outdoor skill, and you will find it useful to know how to follow or draw a simple map. A map is a bird's eye view of an area. It shows you the way to go from one place to another, what the land looks like and where things are. Here and on the next three pages you can find out how to draw a route map, a picture map, and a treasure map.

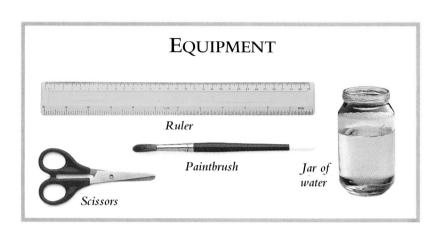

EQUIPMENT

Ruler

Paintbrush

Jar of water

Scissors

You will need

Pocket compass

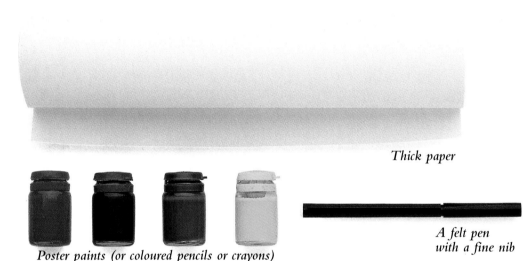

Thick paper

Poster paints (or coloured pencils or crayons)

A felt pen with a fine nib

Notebook and pencil

Simple route map

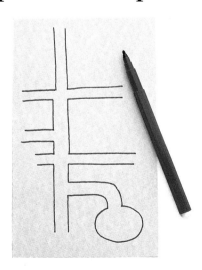

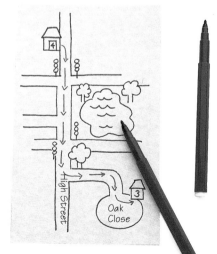

1 Start by drawing the main roads between your home and a friend's house. Show where the smaller side roads join on to them.

2 Draw in the two houses or flats at each end of the route and add any helpful landmarks, such as traffic lights, big trees, or a pond.

3 Write on the house numbers and put in the names of the most important roads. Then draw a line of arrows to show the best route to follow.

Picture map

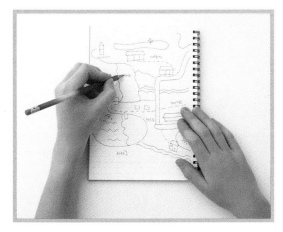

1 Find a spot outdoors with a good view of your chosen area and sketch a map in your notebook, showing all the main landmarks.

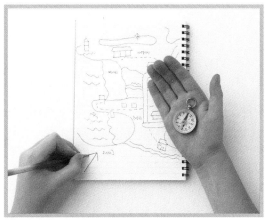

2 Stay in the same place, and find out which way is North with your pocket compass★. Draw an arrow on your map pointing in that direction.

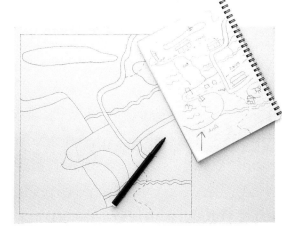

3 Back home, turn the sketch so that the North arrow points straight up and copy the map in this position on to a sheet of paper.

Creating a map key

Most maps use picture symbols to give you information about the area and in one corner there is usually a "key" to tell you what the pictures mean. Make a list of the things you want to show on your map and draw a symbol to represent each one.

Here are some symbols for the sort of things you might want to put on a map of a seaside village.

 Steep hill

 Farmland

 River

 Sea

Sandy beach

 Pebble beach

 Cliff

 Coniferous wood

Deciduous wood

 Footpath

 Road

 Church

 Ice-cream stall

 Café

Telephone box

 Postbox

 Hotel

 Lighthouse

 Bus stop

 Viewpoint

Filling in the details

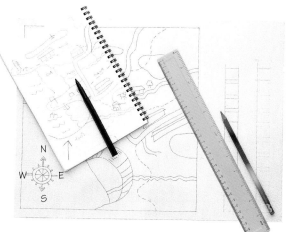

4 In one corner of the map, mark in the points of the compass. Draw boxes for the key picture symbols at one side of the map.

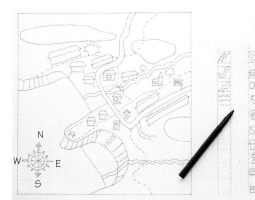

5 Still using your sketch map as reference, draw the picture symbols in place on the map itself and in the boxes for the key.

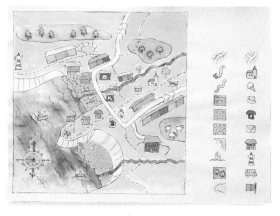

6 Colour in your map making sure the symbols on it match those in the key. Then add place names to the map and label the key symbols.

FINDING THE WAY

The finished route map shows the quickest route between two places. The picture map will also help you to find your way around, but it gives other information as well, so does the treasure island map. To follow a map, turn it so that the symbols on it, especially the paths or roads, line up with what you see in front of you. Then you are ready to set off!

Route map

If someone asks you the way, it is often better to draw a quick map than to try to give directions. Practise drawing route maps to interesting places in your area.

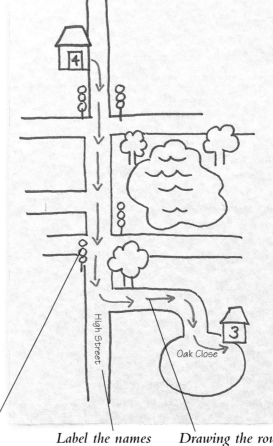

Traffic lights are good landmarks in towns. Make sure you put them in the right place on the map.

Label the names of the main roads to follow on your map.

Drawing the route in a different colour helps to make it clearer.

Picture map

A map like this of a favourite place or a holiday destination is a great record of where you have been, as well as a wonderful picture.

Treasure map

Why not make up your own map of a treasure island? To make it look like an old map, paint the paper with cold, black tea or coffee.

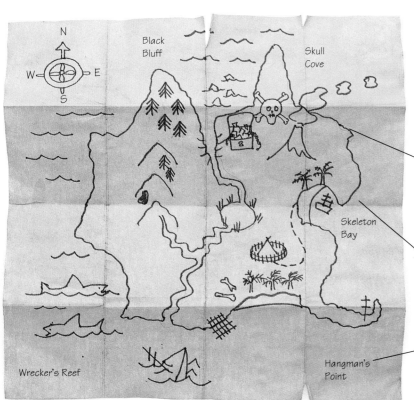

To make your map look even older, try drawing it using a black or brown pen with a thin nib.

Crease the paper several times after drawing the map, to make it look worn.

Make up spooky place names and write them on in old-fashioned looking writing.

Make the compass decorative if you wish. This one is based on a ship's wheel.

Spend a little time making sure that the roads and the coastline are in the right place, and then it will be much easier to fill in the rest of the map.

This map shows two different tree symbols. This one is for deciduous woods and the other for coniferous woods.

Map symbols
Keep the symbols for the map very simple, so that they can be understood at a glance. Make a note of them and try to use the same symbols on all the maps you make.

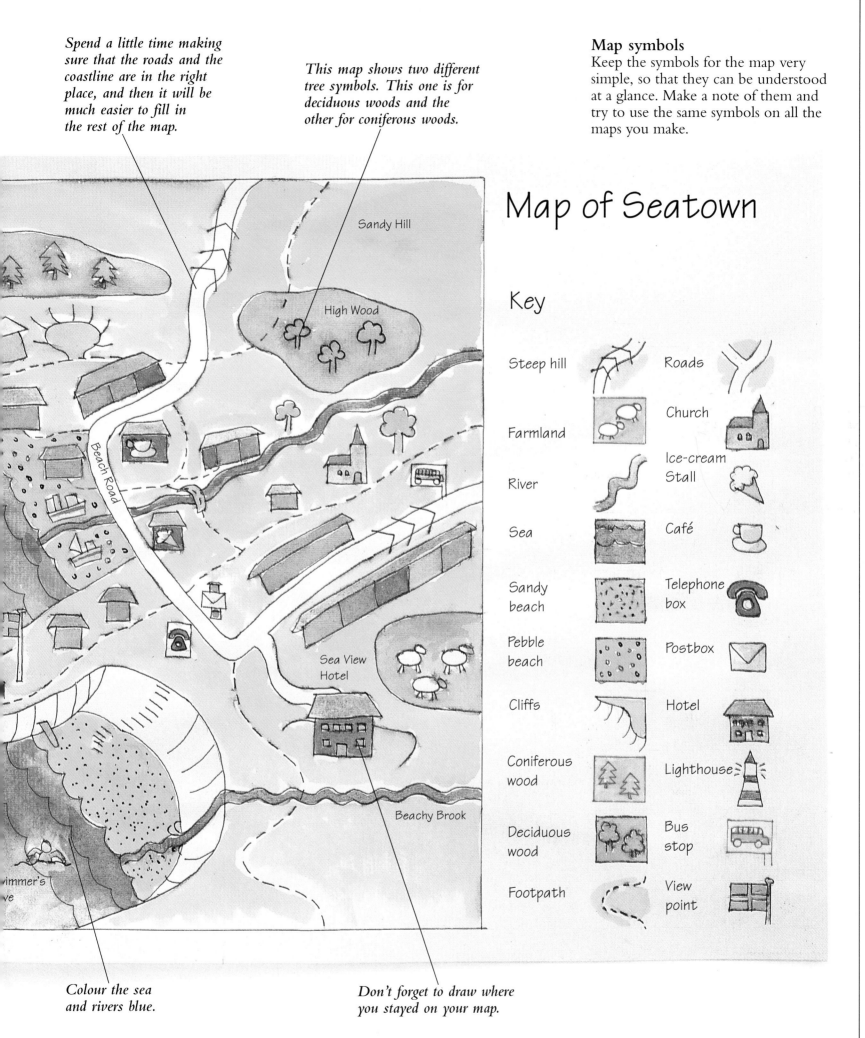

Map of Seatown

Sandy Hill

High Wood

Beach Road

Sea View Hotel

Beachy Brook

immer's ve

Key

Steep hill		Roads	
Farmland		Church	
River		Ice-cream Stall	
Sea		Café	
Sandy beach		Telephone box	
Pebble beach		Postbox	
Cliffs		Hotel	
Coniferous wood		Lighthouse	
Deciduous wood		Bus stop	
Footpath		View point	

Colour the sea and rivers blue.

Don't forget to draw where you stayed on your map.

NATURE MUSEUM

Good nature detectives keep their eyes open for new or interesting finds whenever they are outdoors. Unusual shells, pebbles, leaves, seedheads, stones, and twigs all make good collections to display. Here you can see how to make a tiny chest of drawers and a display showcase for your very own nature museum.

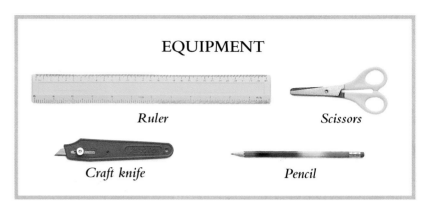

EQUIPMENT

Ruler

Scissors

Craft knife

Pencil

You will need

For the showcase

Thin, white card for labels

Cotton wool

Thick coloured card

The insides of 6 large slotted matchboxes★

For the chest of drawers

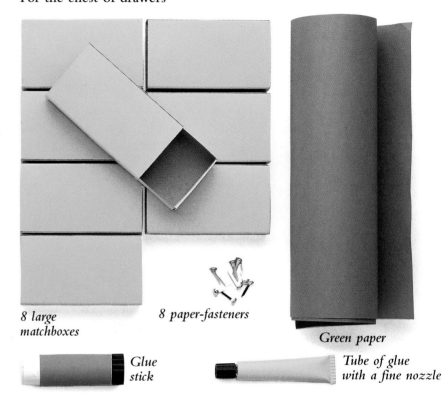

8 large matchboxes

8 paper-fasteners

Green paper

Glue stick

Tube of glue with a fine nozzle

Making the showcase

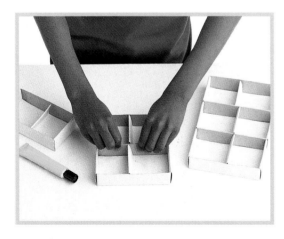

1 Glue three of the matchbox insides together, side by side in a row. Then glue three more box insides together in the same way.

2 Glue the two rows of three boxes together. Fold and glue down the card in the middle of some boxes to make bigger compartments.

3 Ask an adult to cut out a piece of thick card about 3 cm bigger all round than the showcase. Glue the showcase on to the card.

★ *If you can't find slotted matchboxes, glue a small piece of card in the middle of a single matchbox.*

Chest of drawers

1 Glue paper to the front ends of the matchbox insides and push a paper-fastener through each one. Fold the card dividers flat inside the boxes.

2 Glue two of the outer boxes together, side by side. Do this with all the outer boxes, then glue the pairs of boxes on top of each other.

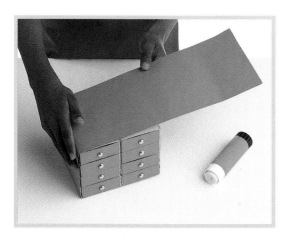

3 Cut a strip of paper as wide as the length of the boxes and long enough to wrap right around them. Glue the paper around the boxes.

Treasures on display

The tiny chest of drawers is a good place to keep natural treasures tucked away. Open the drawers a little if you want to display the contents. The showcase is for larger objects which you want to keep on display all the time.

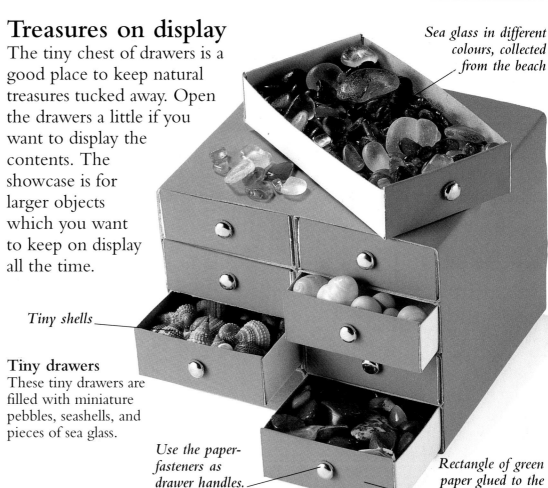

Sea glass in different colours, collected from the beach

Tiny shells

Tiny drawers
These tiny drawers are filled with miniature pebbles, seashells, and pieces of sea glass.

Use the paper-fasteners as drawer handles.

Rectangle of green paper glued to the front of the drawer

Showcase
You can use the showcase for any interesting finds, or keep it for one type of collection, such as shells. Arrange the display to look as attractive as possible.

Line the bottom of each compartment with cotton wool.

Make labels from thin card and glue them on.

New finds
Make your museum more interesting by changing the collection from time to time.

NATURE'S PICTURES

Even if you can't draw, you can create wonderful pictures based on things you find outdoors. Here you can learn how to make collages, pressed-flower pictures, bark rubbings, and paintings. Turn the page to see how to finish and frame the pictures.

EQUIPMENT

Ruler

Scissors

Craft knife

Jar of water

Pencil

Paintbrush

You will need

For pressed-flower and display pictures

Textured paper

A big, heavy book

Blotting paper

Strong glue in a tube

Flowers and leaves, or shells and sea glass

For frames

Coloured card

Masking tape

For tree collage

Textured paper

PVA glue

Leaves, twigs, and sticks

For bark rubbings

Masking tape

Wax crayons

Coloured paper

For water-colour painting

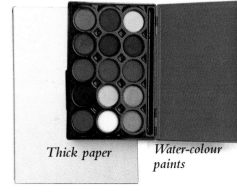

Thick paper

Water-colour paints

For tissue paper collage

White card

Coloured tissue paper

Glue stick

Pressing flowers

1 Open a big book and lay a sheet of blotting paper over it. Arrange the flowers flat on one half of the paper and fold the other half over them.

2 Press more flowers in the same way, further on in the book. Close it up and stack heavy books on top. Leave it for at least four weeks.

Flower picture

Arrange the pressed flowers on a sheet of paper. Then dab a tiny spot of glue on the back of each flower and gently stick it down in position.

Seashore picture

You can make a picture from a seashore collection. Arrange your treasures on a sheet of paper. Dab strong glue on the back of each item and stick it down.

Tree collage

1 Stick the paper to card to keep it firm. Glue on a stick for a tree trunk and twigs for branches. Add dead leaves around the bottom.

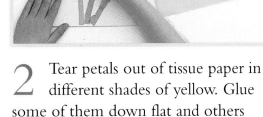

2 Fill in the rest of the tree with clusters of fresh green leaves to look like the leaves of the tree. You may need quite a lot of glue.

Tissue paper collage

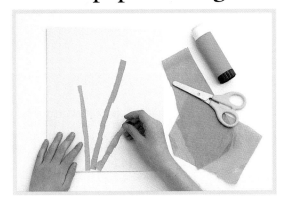

1 Cut some strips of tissue paper to make the stems of the flowers. Gently glue them to the paper and smooth out any wrinkles.

2 Tear petals out of tissue paper in different shades of yellow. Glue some of them down flat and others just at one end, to look ruffled.

Bark rubbings

1 Find a tree with fairly smooth bark and no moss or lichen growing on it. Tape a piece of paper firmly to the tree trunk.

2 Use the flat side of a wax crayon and rub it firmly up and down, to mark the bark pattern on the paper. Then untape the paper.

Flower painting

1 Put the flower you are painting in front of you and draw it as carefully as you can. Keep looking at the real flower to see what it is like.

2 Then paint the flower. Keep to one colour at a time and let each colour dry before painting the next so that they don't run together.

PICTURE GALLERY

Making a frame

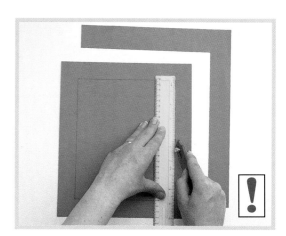

1 Measure the height and width of the picture. Add 3 cm all the way around to give you the size of the outside edges of the frame.

2 Draw the rectangular outer frame on card. Then measure and draw another rectangle inside the first, each side 4 cm smaller than the outer frame.

3 To make the frame, ask an adult to cut along both the inner and outer rectangles for you, using a ruler and a craft knife.

Nature exhibition

Hang the finished pictures up in your room, or beside your nature museum. Change your display through the year as the seasons change.

Daffodil pictures
Why not try using different techniques to make pictures of the same subject?

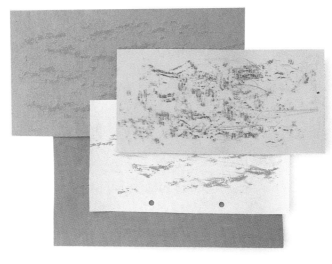

Bark rubbings
Try doing rubbings on different coloured papers, and using chalks as well as wax crayons, to create different effects. Write the name of the tree the rubbing comes from on the back of the paper.

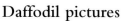

The loose petals on this tissue paper collage give the flower a three-dimensional effect.

This picture of a daffodil in a blue jug was painted using watercolour paints.

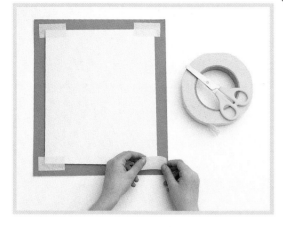

4 Lay your picture face down on the back of the frame, making sure the picture is centered, and then tape the picture to the frame.

Fresh leaves

Branches made from twigs

Dead leaves and twigs, for the ground

Trunk made from a stick

Tree collage
Pictures like this are best displayed on a flat surface, rather than hung up. The picture will last until the fresh leaves begin to wilt.

Shells

Sea glass

Shell collages
Collections like this work best if you keep the rows of objects simple and keep similar colours together. You could try arranging your shells into a picture, instead.

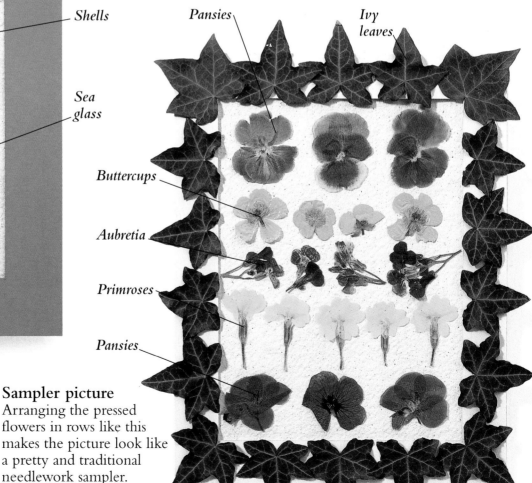

Pansies

Ivy leaves

Buttercups

Aubretia

Primroses

Pansies

Sampler picture
Arranging the pressed flowers in rows like this makes the picture look like a pretty and traditional needlework sampler.

WEATHER STATION

Is it going to be hot or cold today? Will it rain or stay dry? The weather changes all the time, but you can learn to spot the signs of what it might do next. Here you can find out how to set up your own weather station and keep a record of the weather each day. Below you can see how to make a raincatcher and a wind vane. Overleaf you can find out how to use them and keep a weather chart.

EQUIPMENT

Ruler

Small hammer

Scissors

Felt pen

Pocket compass

Craft knife

You will need

For the wind vane

Strong glue with a fine nozzle

Pin

A piece of dowelling about 25 cm long

A plastic tub with a lid

A plastic drinking straw

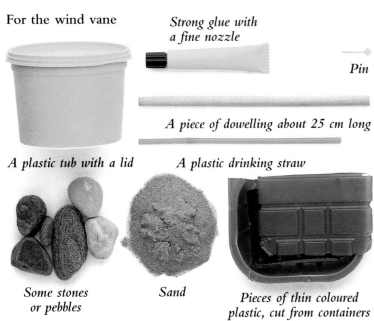

Some stones or pebbles

Sand

Pieces of thin coloured plastic, cut from containers

For the raincatcher

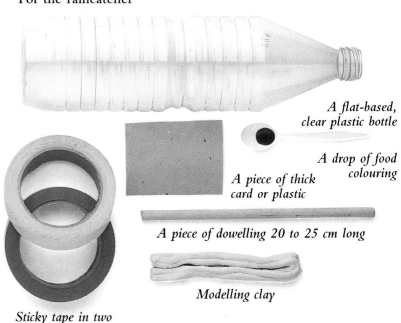

A flat-based, clear plastic bottle

A drop of food colouring

A piece of thick card or plastic

A piece of dowelling 20 to 25 cm long

Sticky tape in two different colours

Modelling clay

Making the raincatcher

1 Cut off the bottom half of the bottle. Then cut off the funnel part of the top of the bottle. You will not need the middle section.

2 Slide the top part of the bottle upside down into the base of the bottle, to act like a funnel. Stick the bottle edges together with tape.

3 Roll the modelling clay into a long sausage and press it around the base of the raincatcher. Use this to hold the raincatcher in place outside.

4 Put a drop of food colouring into the bottle, so that the rainwater you catch will be coloured and you will be able to see it clearly.

5 To make a dipstick, hold the piece of dowelling against a ruler. Use a felt pen to make centimetre marks along half of the stick.

6 For decoration, wind sticky tape around the top part of the stick. Cut a cloud shape out of card, colour it, and tape it to the top of the stick.

Making the wind vane

1 Make a hole in the lid of the plastic tub with a craft knife. Wind sticky tape, in two colours, around the dowelling to decorate it.

2 Hold the stick upright in the centre of the tub and fill the tub with stones and sand. Slide the lid over the stick and press it on to the tub.

3 Cut four small triangles out of coloured plastic. Then cut out two bigger triangles and two large "V" shapes, as shown in the picture.

4 Glue the four small triangles to the lid of the tub in opposite pairs so that they are pointing in four different directions.

5 Glue the two large triangles together to cover one end of the straw. Glue the "V" shapes together to cover the other end of the straw.

6 Using a hammer, pin the straw to the top of the stick with the map pin so that the straw lies level and can spin freely in the wind.

WEATHER WATCH

Once you have made the raincatcher and wind vane, you will need to buy a simple thermometer to complete your weather station. Then draw up a weather chart and try to keep a daily record of the weather by studying the sky and using your instruments.

Tape on a piece of ribbon to hang up your chart.

Weather chart

Make a weather chart by drawing a grid, like the one shown below, on some sheets of paper. Use paper-fasteners to pin the grids on to a rectangle of stiff card. Draw the weather symbols you are going to use on a strip of paper and glue it along the bottom of the card.

Unfasten the top sheet of paper at the end of each week to give you a new chart for the next week.

Glue on a strip of paper and make a decorative heading.

Paper-fasteners hold the grids in place on the card

Weather Chart

Week beginning 25 May	Sunday	Monday	Tuesday	Wednesday	Thursday	Friday	Saturday
Temperature	21°C	18°C	17°C	17°C	19°C		
Wind direction	SW	SW	W	W	NW		
Rainfall	O	O	O	1 cm	0.5 cm		
Weather conditions							

Weather symbols	Clear sky	Some cloud	Cloudy	Windy	Thunder	Rain	Snow	Hail

Use these picture symbols, or make some up, to show what the weather is like.

You could add more symbols to show fog, mist, or frost.

Weather station

Set up your weather station outside and use the instruments to find out how much rain falls, what the temperature is, and which way the wind is blowing. Record your findings on your weather chart.

This thermometer shows the temperature in two scales, degrees Celsius (°C) and Fahrenheit (°F).

The top of the blue column of liquid moves up and down to show the air temperature.

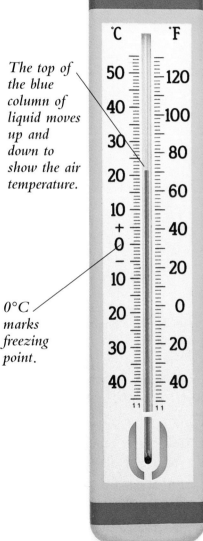

0°C marks freezing point.

Raincatcher

Stand the raincatcher in an open space (without its dipstick). Fix it in place with the modelling clay and check every day to see whether there is any rainwater in it. If there is, dip the stick into it and measure the amount of water.

Put the dipstick upright in the raincatcher.

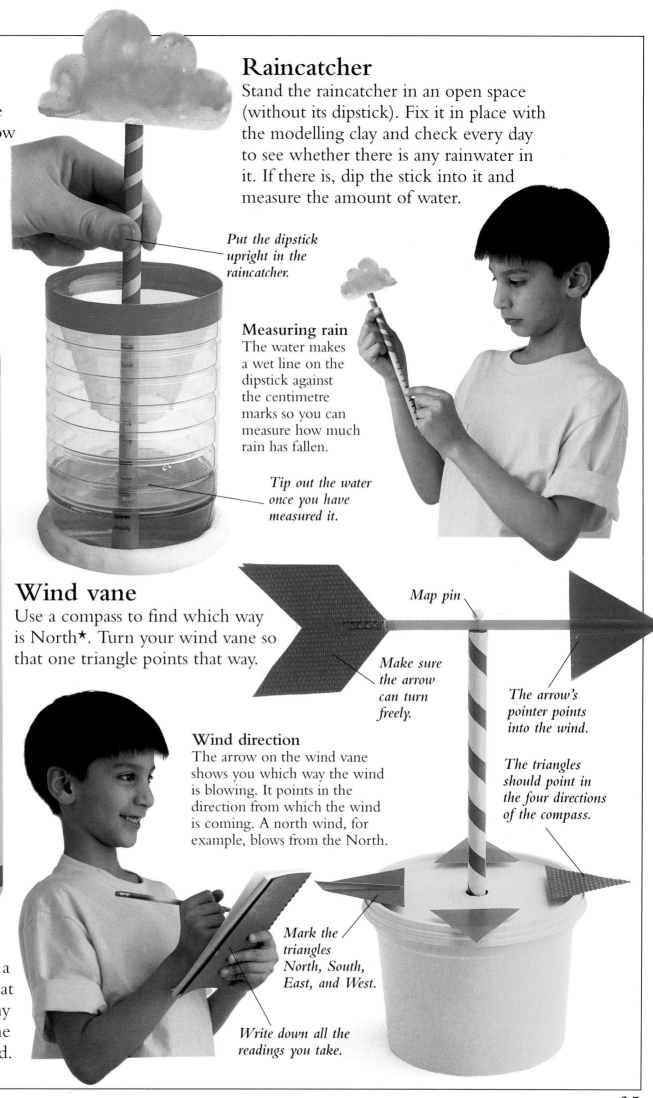

Measuring rain
The water makes a wet line on the dipstick against the centimetre marks so you can measure how much rain has fallen.

Tip out the water once you have measured it.

Wind vane

Use a compass to find which way is North★. Turn your wind vane so that one triangle points that way.

Map pin

Make sure the arrow can turn freely.

The arrow's pointer points into the wind.

Wind direction
The arrow on the wind vane shows you which way the wind is blowing. It points in the direction from which the wind is coming. A north wind, for example, blows from the North.

The triangles should point in the four directions of the compass.

Mark the triangles North, South, East, and West.

Thermometer

Hang the thermometer in a shady place outside. Look at it at the same time each day and read the number by the top of the column of liquid.

Write down all the readings you take.

★See page 62.

PLANT A GARDEN

You don't need much space to have a garden. Here and on the next page you can see how to plant a colourful garden of flowers and herbs on a plot that is only one metre square. For an instant garden, use bedding plants (colourful plants which last one summer) mixed with a few longer lasting ones. Or sow seeds in trays in spring and plant them out in the garden in early summer.

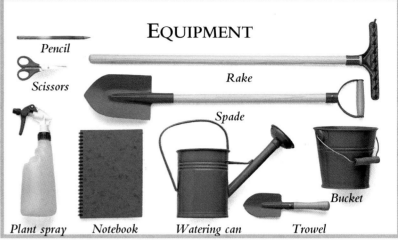

EQUIPMENT

Pencil

Scissors

Rake

Spade

Plant spray   Notebook   Watering can   Trowel   Bucket

You will need

An attractive pot for the centrepiece

2 purple sage plants

2 variegated oregano plants

4 golden feverfew, or golden marjoram plants

2 sweet basil plants

1 thyme plant

20 small, purple viola plants

2 pink-flowered strawberry plants

4 white marguerite plants

1 large, pink, perennial geranium plant

4 large yellow viola plants

2 lilac petunia plants

4 pink dianthus plants

Planting out

1 Decide where you are going to put a plant and dig a hole a little deeper than the plant's container. Check that the hole is big enough.

2 To take a plant out of a pot, tip the plant upside down between your fingers and squeeze the pot at the sides to loosen the compost.

3 Stand the plant in the hole you have dug. Fill in the spaces around it with soil and press the soil down. Then water the plant well.

Planning the garden

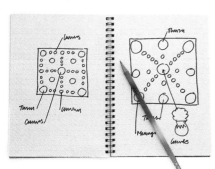

Look at other gardens for ideas. Then draw a plan based on a simple pattern and decide which plants to use.

Preparing the ground

First of all, working from the middle to the edges of the plot, take out the weeds (make sure that you remove all their roots, too). Dig over the ground, to break up the soil. Then dig in some garden compost to improve the soil. Finally, rake the soil level.

Arranging the plants

1 Put the centrepiece in place, then plant the lines of plants that form the framework of your design.

When you design your garden, always try to choose plants in colours that go well together.

2 Fill in the rest of the garden with plants. Allow enough space around each plant for it to grow.

GARDEN IN BLOOM

The finished garden

Once you have finished creating your garden, it is important to look after the plants all year round. By following the simple steps below you will have a healthy and long-lasting garden. Before buying any plants, check the labels to see what conditions they grow best in.

Watering

Water the plants every day, unless it rains, until they have settled in and started growing. After that just water them if the soil looks dry.

Pest control

Check the garden regularly for signs of pests. Remove snails, and spray green or blackfly with a mixture of warm water and washing-up liquid.

Dead-heading

Plants will flower for longer if you regularly pick or snip off the dead flower heads. Snip the herbs often, to keep them small and bushy.

Gathering herbs

Once your herbs have grown, pick their leaves to cook with. If you used the pink-flowering strawberry plants, the fruit may taste slightly bitter.

Spring bulbs

For a pretty Spring garden, plant Spring-flowering bulbs between the plants. Plant them in Autumn following any instructions.

A white marguerite is planted at each corner.

Golden marjoram

Dianthus

Lilac and yellow viola

Pink-flowering strawberry plant

Lilac petunia

Matching plants are placed each side of the feverfew.

Pick the leaves of sweet basil regularly. It goes very well with tomato dishes.

Small purple violas form the lines of the cross. Deadhead and trim them regularly, to keep the lines in shape.

Lilac viola

Purple sage is planted on each side of the central pot.

Golden feverfew produces small, daisy-like flowers.

Yellow viola

Brick edging

This thyme has green and yellow lemon-scented leaves and purple flowers.

Ornamental pot containing a pink geranium

Variegated oregano has small pink flowers in Summer. You can use the leaves to flavour pasta dishes.

GIANTS FROM SEEDS

Why not see if you can grow a giant plant from a tiny seed? Sunflowers and pumpkins can both grow to a huge size, if they have the right conditions – and you are patient. Read the seed packets to check they are the giant varieties. Then have a competition with a friend, to see who can grow the tallest sunflower or the biggest pumpkin!

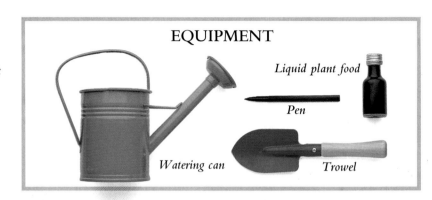

EQUIPMENT

Liquid plant food

Pen

Watering can

Trowel

You will need

Plant labels

Elastic bands

Sunflower seeds, giant variety

Pumpkin seeds, giant variety

Seed compost

Garden canes

8 cm flower pots with drip trays

Plastic bags

Planting pumpkins

1 Fill the pots with compost and push two or three seeds about 2 cm into it. Water the pots well and label the seeds.

2 Secure plastic bags over the pots with an elastic band and place on a light window-sill. When the first shoots appear, remove the bags.

3 After danger of frost is past, pull out all but the strongest seedling in each pot. Plant the strong seedlings in the garden and water them.

Sowing sunflowers

1 Plant three seeds in each place where you want one plant, as they will not all grow. Push the seeds about 1 cm down into the soil.

2 Label the seeds and water them well. As the seedlings grow, pull out any weak ones, so the plants are about 45 cm apart. Support small seedlings with garden canes.

Golden giants

Pumpkins are trailing plants and will need at least two metres each in which to grow. Harvest your pumpkins 12 to 20 weeks after they have been planted.

They are ripe when the skin hardens and the stem cracks. Cut them off their plants and stand them in a bright place for 10 days, so the skin hardens further.

Mighty flowers

Sunflowers can grow up to three metres tall. To stop them from falling over, tie each sunflower to a garden cane as it grows taller. Measure the plants every week and keep a record of their heights in your nature log book.

If you want a really tall plant, pinch out any side shoots as they appear. When the seeds are ripe, cut off the sunflower heads, keep the seeds, and save them for planting the following year.

Once the skin has hardened, use your pumpkin for cooking, or scoop out the inside and use the hollow shell as a candle holder.

BIRD TABLE

The best way to find out about birds is to put out food for them so that you can watch them at close hand. Here and over the page you can find out how to make a bird table, gourmet bird food, and some nifty feeders. You will need an adult's help to make the bird table.

EQUIPMENT

For the bird tables

Small hammer

Ruler

Large hammer

Paintbrush

Sticky tape

Scissors

Pencil

Craft knife

For the bird feed

Small saucepan

Large needle

Wooden spoon

Bowl

You will need
For the bird table

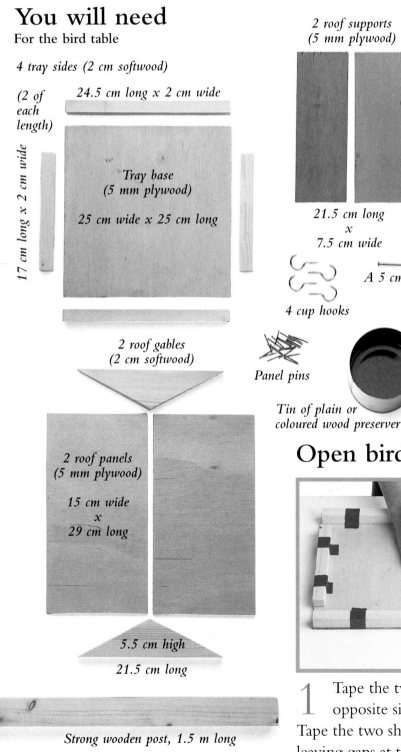

4 tray sides (2 cm softwood)

(2 of each length)

24.5 cm long x 2 cm wide

17 cm long x 2 cm wide

Tray base (5 mm plywood)

25 cm wide x 25 cm long

2 roof supports (5 mm plywood)

21.5 cm long x 7.5 cm wide

A 5 cm nail

4 cup hooks

Panel pins

Tin of plain or coloured wood preserver

2 roof gables (2 cm softwood)

2 roof panels (5 mm plywood)

15 cm wide x 29 cm long

5.5 cm high

21.5 cm long

Strong wooden post, 1.5 m long

For bird pudding feeders

Porridge oats

Birdseed

Cooked vegetables

Dried fruit

Large fir cone

Cooked rice

Breadcrumbs

Nuts (not salted)

100 g lard

Small yogurt carton

Forked twig

For the carton feeder

Small milk carton

For the peanut feeder

Peanuts in their shells

Garden twine

Open bird table

1 Tape the two longer tray sides to opposite sides of the tray base. Tape the two shorter sides in place, leaving gaps at the corners.

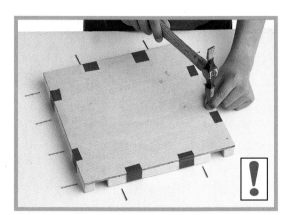

2 Turn the tray over. Nail the base of the tray to the tray sides with panel pins, using a small hammer*. Then peel off the tape.

 ★ See page 62.

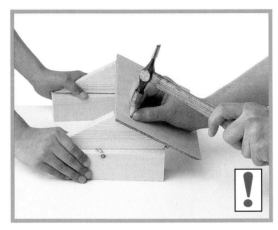

3 Draw diagonal lines across the tray to find the centre. Ask an adult to nail the tray to the post with a 5 cm nail, where the lines cross.

4 Screw two cup hooks into each of the longer sides of the tray. Then ask an adult to set up the bird table in the garden (see page 45).

1 Follow steps 1 and 2 for the open bird table. Then measure and draw a pencil line 2 cm in from each side of the two roof pieces.

2 Rest the roof gables on blocks of wood. Nail the roof panels on to the gables, lining up the gables inside the pencil lines you have drawn.

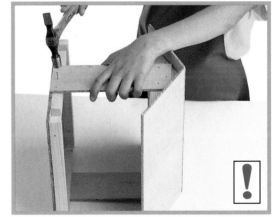

3 Hold the roof against a table. Nail one of the roof supports to the centre of a gable with panel pins. Do the same at the other side.

4 Stand the tray and roof on their sides. Nail the roof supports to the outer edges of the short tray sides. Then nail the tray to the post★.

Yogurt pot feeder

1 Melt the lard in a saucepan over a low heat. Put the rest of the food in a bowl and pour the melted lard over it. Mix it in well.

2 Spoon the pudding mixture into the yogurt pot. Push the twig into the mixture, then leave the pudding until it sets hard.

3 When the pudding has set, pull it out of the yogurt pot by the twig and roll it in birdseed. Tie a piece of string to the twig.

★*Ask an adult to do this, as in Step 3 for the Open bird table.*

BIRD WATCH

Peanut feeder

Thread a big needle with a double length of garden twine. Knot the ends of the twine together, then thread the peanuts on to it.

Milk carton feeder

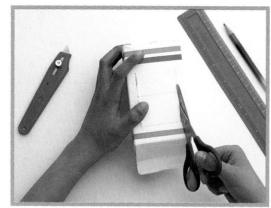

1 Draw a rectangle, with a line across it a third of the way up, on the front of the carton. Cut along the sides and top of the rectangle.

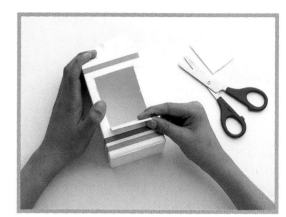

2 Cut along the middle line and bend back the flap along the bottom line of the rectangle. Do the same on the back of the carton.

Bird patrol

The more you watch birds, the easier it will become to recognize common ones. Find out which birds visit your local area first, then try bird spotting in woods, by a river, or by the sea. It helps to make quick sketches. Look out for a bird's colour, size, the shape of its beak, wings, and feet, and any special features.

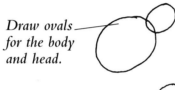

Draw ovals for the body and head.

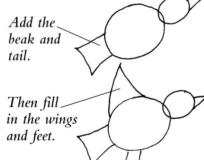

Add the beak and tail.

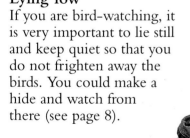

Then fill in the wings and feet.

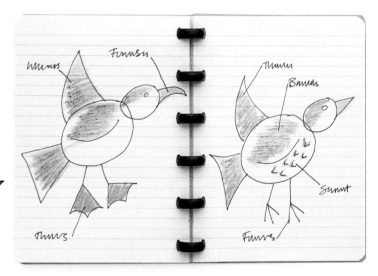

Lying low

If you are bird-watching, it is very important to lie still and keep quiet so that you do not frighten away the birds. You could make a hide and watch from there (see page 8).

What was it?

If you don't recognize a bird, draw a sketch of it and make some notes to help you look it up in a field guide back at home.

A closer look

It is a good idea to carry binoculars with you so that you can look closely at any birds you see.

Feeding the birds

Ask an adult to set the bird table up in the garden for you and paint it with wood preservative. Make sure there are no hiding places nearby where cats might lie in wait. Then hang up the feeders you have made and put out some tasty titbits!

This bird table has been stained with green wood preservative to stop it from rotting.

Stale cakes, bread, and biscuits, old cheese, bacon rinds, and unsalted nuts are all good scraps for birds.

The gaps at the corners of the table let any rainwater drain away.

Open bird table
You can add any of the feeders to the open bird table, in the same way as for the covered one. Check the food on this table after it has rained, and replace anything that has gone soggy.

Fir-cone feeder
Push bird pudding into the cracks of a large fir-cone to make this feeder.

Yogurt pot feeder
Hang this feeder from the bird table and watch the birds sway as they feed from it.

Peanut feeder
Tie up the peanut feeder and watch the birds crack open the nuts with their beaks.

Carton feeder
Make a hole in the top of the carton feeder and tie string through it. Fill the feeder with birdseed.

This flap makes a perch for the birds to stand on as they feed.

IN CLOSE-UP

All around you, on the ground, in the water, and in the air, under your very nose, tiny creatures are busily leading their own lives. To find out more about these minibeasts, you will need to collect some and take a closer look. Here and over the page you can find out how to make four useful pieces of equipment: a collecting jar, a water viewer, a fishing net, and an amazing insect catcher called a pooter.

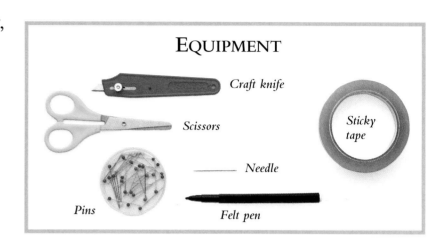

EQUIPMENT

Craft knife

Scissors

Sticky tape

Needle

Pins

Felt pen

You will need

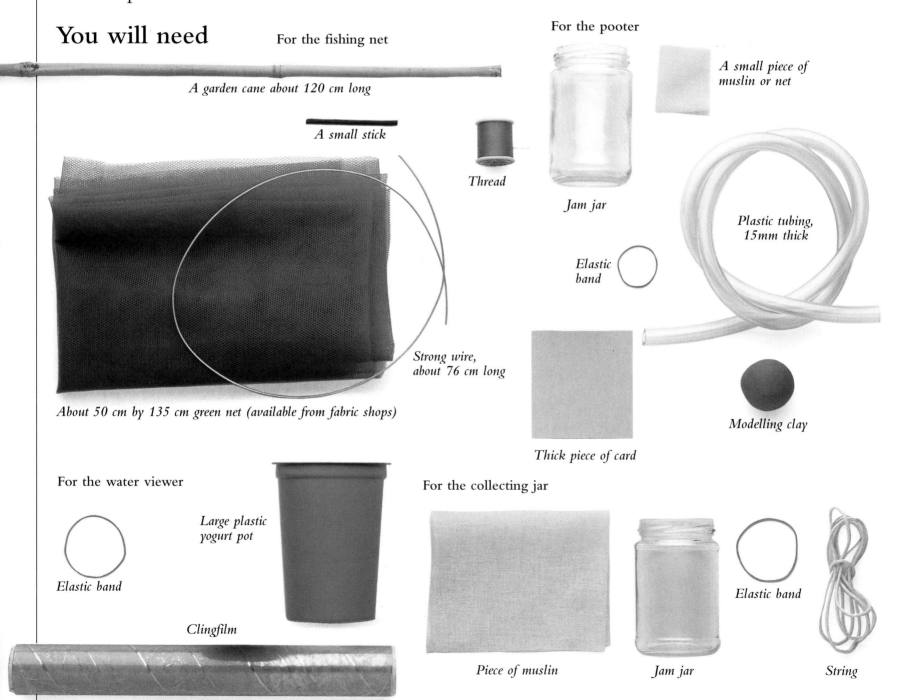

For the fishing net

A garden cane about 120 cm long

A small stick

Thread

About 50 cm by 135 cm green net (available from fabric shops)

Strong wire, about 76 cm long

For the pooter

A small piece of muslin or net

Jam jar

Plastic tubing, 15mm thick

Elastic band

Thick piece of card

Modelling clay

For the water viewer

Elastic band

Large plastic yogurt pot

Clingfilm

For the collecting jar

Piece of muslin

Jam jar

Elastic band

String

Collecting jar

 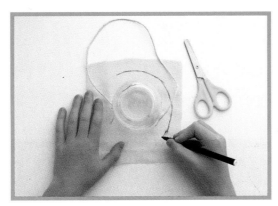 

1 Tie a long piece of string round the neck of the jar, leaving a long end free. Tie the free end across the jar to make a handle as shown.

2 Stand the jar on a piece of muslin. With a felt pen, draw a circle about 2 cm bigger than the base of the jar round it.

3 Cut out the circle of muslin. Lay it on top of the jar and stretch it flat. Then fasten it in place around the neck of the jar with an elastic band.

Fishing net

 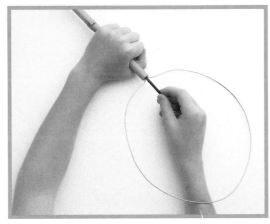 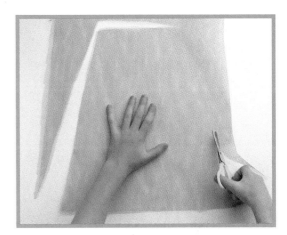

1 Bend the piece of wire into a circle, then bend out the wire about 4 cm from each end, as shown, to form two prongs.

2 Push the two prongs of the wire circle into the hollow end of the garden cane. Push a small stick into the cane to wedge the wire in place.

3 Fold the net in half. Cut out two bucket-shaped pieces from the net, about 36 cm deep, 37 cm wide at the top and 24 cm wide at the bottom.

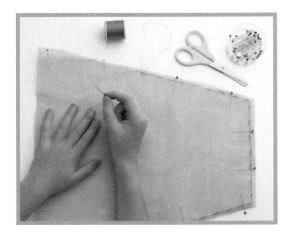  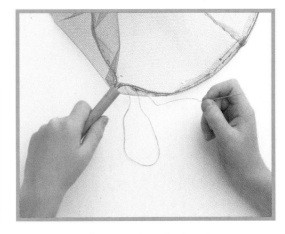

4 Pin the pieces of net together around three sides, leaving the top open. Sew along the pinned sides, 1 cm in from the edges, in backstitch.★

5 Remove the pins and turn the net inside out. Fold the top of the net over the wire loop and pin it in place all the way around.

6 Sew the net firmly in place, using backstitch★, starting and finishing with double stitches★ next to the cane. Finally, remove the pins.

★Ask an adult to help you with this.

MINIBEAST PATROL

Water viewer

1 Ask an adult to cut out the bottom of the yogurt pot very carefully, using a craft knife. Do not try to do this yourself.

2 Cut out a large circle of clingfilm. Stretch it over the top of the yogurt pot and fasten it tightly in place with an elastic band.

Pooter

1 Draw a circle round the top of the jam jar on to the card. Inside this circle, draw two smaller circles round the tubing. Cut out the circles.

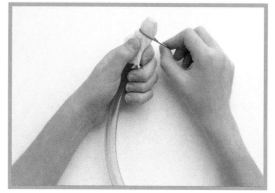

2 Cut the tubing into two pieces 25 cm long and 50 cm long. Tie a piece of muslin over one end of the short tube with an elastic band.

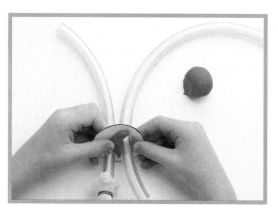

3 Push the two pieces of tubing through the holes in the card circle. Wedge them both in place underneath with modelling clay.

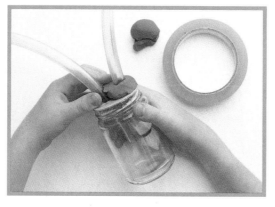

4 Fasten the circle of card to the top of the jar with tape, then press modelling clay over the top of the card, to hold the tubes in place.

Bug watch

Take your fishing net, collecting jar, water viewer, and pooter to different habitats, such as meadows, woods, ponds, or the seashore to look for mini wildlife. It is a good idea to take a magnifying glass, notebook, and pencil with you, too.

Kindness, not cruelty

Remember – minibeasts are living creatures, so treat them kindly. Only keep them for as long as you have to, study them and make notes, then gently put them back where you found them. Always wash your hands after touching pond water, animals, or soil.

Suck in air through the end of this tube.

Remove the muslin cover to put an insect in the jar, then tie the cover on again.

Collecting jar

String handle

Examining minibeasts

You can use the collecting jar to examine creatures you find on land, such as this spider. You can also use it to house water creatures you catch with the fishing net. However, you must fill the jar with water from the place where you are fishing, so that the animals can breathe.

Viewing end

Water sight
The edges of ponds, streams, and rock pools are all good places to look for minibeasts, but take great care on slippery banks and rocks, and make sure there is an adult with you at all times. To use the water viewer, dip the plastic-covered end a few centimetres into the water and look through the hole. You should get a good view of life below the surface of the water.

Clingfilm screen

Water viewer

Fishing net

Garden cane handle

Net

Wire hoop

What have I found?
Study each creature you find. What is it doing? Can you see the creature's head? Does it have eyes or antennae? How many legs and wings has it got, and how many parts to its body? Do a quick sketch of each creature you find.

Underwater search
Use your fishing net in ponds, streams, or rock pools. Try sweeping it over the surface of the water to see what you find, then try collecting lower down. You could also try scooping up mud and stones from the bottom, but take care not to rip your net. Do you find different minibeasts at each level?

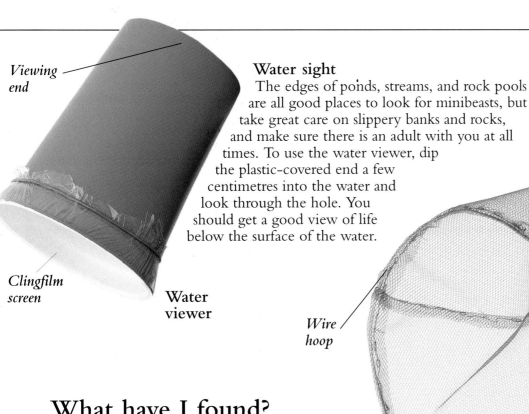

Hold this end above the insect you want to catch.

Modelling clay holds the tubes in place.

Muslin cover stops insects being sucked into your mouth.

What is a pooter?
A pooter is a clever device for collecting small insects into a jar without touching them. Once inside the jar, you can study them at close range.

Using a pooter
Hold the longer tube just above the insect. Then suck on the short tube, and the insect will whoosh up into the jar. Untape the lid to release it.

NATURE LOG BOOK

Your nature log book is your own record of all the things you see, find, and collect on your expeditions outdoors. You can draw in it, stick in unusual treasures, put in pressed plants, magazine cuttings, or photographs you have taken, and keep records of surveys or experiments you have done. To make your log book really special, why not make the book yourself with different sorts of card and paper? Below you can see what to do.

The cover
Stick a picture on to the cover and add a torn paper square for the title.

Roughly knot the raffia, to give the book a natural look.

Sam's
Nature
Log book

Choose a stick slightly longer than the height of the book.

Draw a picture to stick on to the front cover of your book.

EQUIPMENT

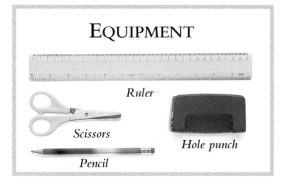

Ruler

Scissors

Hole punch

Pencil

You will need

Raffia

2 sheets of thick, coloured card

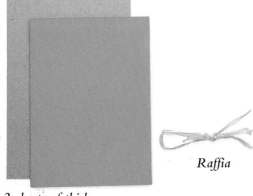

A variety of sheets of paper and tracing paper

A straight stick

Making the log book

1 Cut two rectangles of card for the cover. For the pages, cut the paper into slightly smaller rectangles. Punch holes through all the sheets as shown.

2 Put the paper inside the covers, lining up the holes. Tie pieces of raffia through the holes and around the stick, to hold the book together.

Expedition notebook
The notes you make in your expedition notebook will provide lots of material for your log book. Copy things out giving details of the dates and places.

Collections
Things you have collected can be taped and glued into your log book.

Pages made with paper of different textures and colours, make the log book look interesting.

Catkins

Pussy-willow

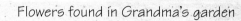

Flowers found in Grandma's garden

ird table survey						
ood		Mon	Tue	Wed	Thur	Fri
ple		2	3			
ed feeder		6	4			
d pudding		3	4			
eadcrumbs		15				
eese		4				

Giant daisy

Aubretia

Pansies

Buttercups

Song thrush seen in Grandma's garden on Sunday

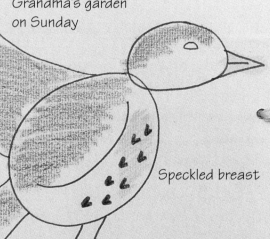

Speckled breast

Plastic envelope of seeds collected

Collect pictures of birds and insects.

Bird study
Copy any sketches you make outdoors (see page 44), filling in as much detail and colour as you can from your notes.

Small flower press to take on expeditions

Plant file
Your nature log book is a good place to keep pressed flowers and leaves (see page 28)★. Stick them in gently with glue and cover them with a sheet of tracing paper to protect them.

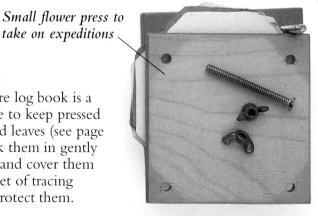

★Remember – never pick or uproot wild plants.

MAKE A KITE

Why not make your own kite with a tail and paint it in bold colours to stand out against the sky? The kite is made of thin plastic, so look out for a large, brightly coloured plastic bag or bin liner with no writing on it. To decorate the kite you will need acrylic paints or marker pens. Turn the page to see how to finish the kite and send it flying!

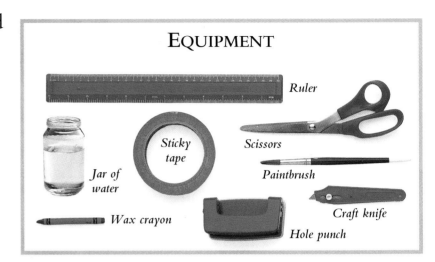

EQUIPMENT

Ruler

Scissors

Sticky tape

Paintbrush

Jar of water

Wax crayon

Craft knife

Hole punch

You will need

A large plastic bag or bin liner

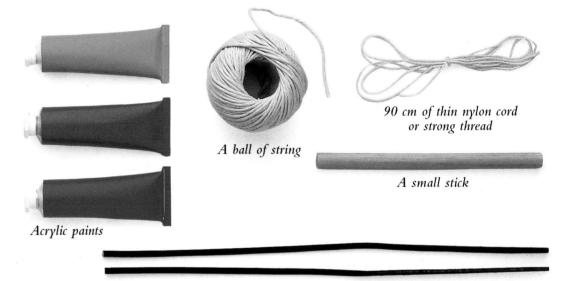

Acrylic paints

A ball of string

90 cm of thin nylon cord or strong thread

A small stick

2 garden canes, 46 cm long

What to do

1 Cut out a square of plastic, 48 cm wide. Mark the centre of the square top and bottom and make three marks, in a line, 14 cm from the top.

2 Draw straight lines to join up the marks at the edges of the plastic square. Cut carefully along the lines keeping the plastic flat.

3 Stick two strips of tape across all the corners of the kite, both back and front, to strengthen them. Trim the pieces of tape to fit the corners.

4 Fold over each corner of the kite in turn, and punch a hole through the double thickness, to make two holes next to each other, as shown.

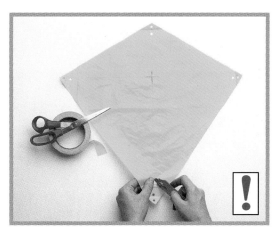

5 Stick tape strips to the centre of the kite, 11 cm from the top and 7 cm from the bottom. Ask an adult to cut a small slit in these taped patches.

6 Paint the front of the kite with acrylic paints, to decorate it. Keep your design bold and simple and do not let the colours run. Leave the kite to dry.

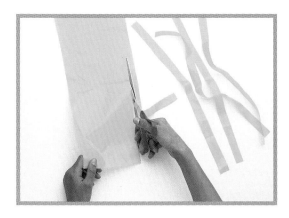

7 Cut about eight ribbons of thin plastic all the same length. Hold the ribbons together and punch a hole through one end of them.

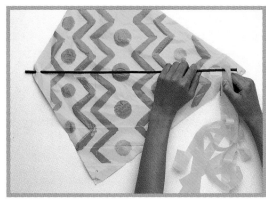

8 Push the end of one garden stick through the holes in the top of the kite. Thread the kite tail ribbons on to the other end of the stick.

9 Tape the top end of the stick in place. Push the other end of the stick through the holes at the bottom of the kite and tape that in place, too.

10 Push the ends of the second stick through the side holes in the kite. Tape it in place in the same way, pulling the plastic tight.

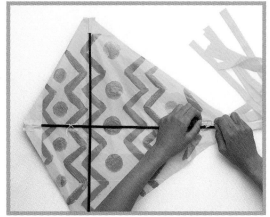

11 Thread the ends of the cord through the slits in the kite, from the painted side. Knot each end on to the stick at the back of the kite.

12 Turn the kite over and tie a small loop in the cord. The loop should be directly over the top slit when you pull the cord up tight.

FLYING HIGH

Making the handle

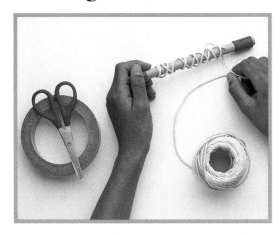

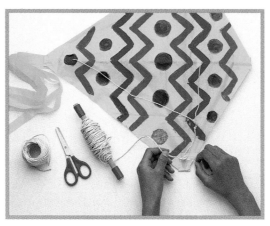

1 Wrap sticky tape around each end of the small stick. Tie one end of the ball of string to the stick, then wind on about 30 metres of string.

2 Tie the loose end of the string through the loop in the thread at the front of the kite. Knot it twice to make sure it is secure.

Flying well
Move the position of the loop in the thread if the kite does not fly as well as you want it to.

Flying the kite

Wait for a windy day to fly your kite, then look for an open space, away from any trees, buildings, overhead cables or roads. Ask a friend to go with you to help you to launch the kite.

Crash landings
If the kite dives and crashes, rewind most of the string before you try to launch it again.

Launching the kite
Stand with your back to the wind and unwind a few metres of the kite string. Ask your friend to carry the kite away from you, holding it up into the wind, and keeping the string pulled tight. Give the order to toss the kite up into the air. As it goes up, start letting out more string.

Keep tugging on the string to keep it tight and the kite should rise into the air.

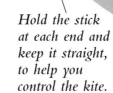

Hold the stick at each end and keep it straight, to help you control the kite.

Kite designs

You could decorate your kite with a sun design, a giant butterfly or any ideas of your own. You could also make a multicoloured tail for it.

The looped thread is always at the front of the kite.

Kite tails
If the kite keeps nose-diving, try making a longer tail for it.

The kite tail helps to keep it steady in the air.

Make sure the plastic is stretched quite tightly against the sticks on the back of it, to keep the kite firm.

TINY BOATS

You may know a pond, a bubbling stream or a rockpool which would be good for sailing model boats. If so, try out your boat-building skills and make a boat that really sails in the wind. Below you can find out how to make a mini-raft and a colourful catamaran from bits and pieces you can find around your home or garden. Ask an adult to go with you when you play near water.

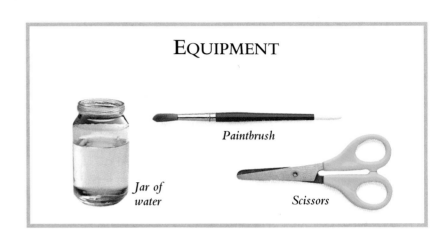

EQUIPMENT

Paintbrush

Jar of water

Scissors

You will need

For the raft

For the catamaran

For sails for both boats

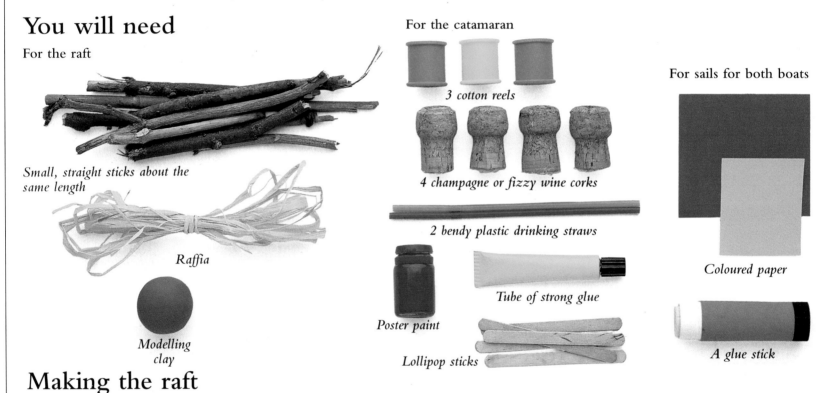

Small, straight sticks about the same length

3 cotton reels

4 champagne or fizzy wine corks

2 bendy plastic drinking straws

Coloured paper

Raffia

Poster paint

Tube of strong glue

Modelling clay

Lollipop sticks

A glue stick

Making the raft

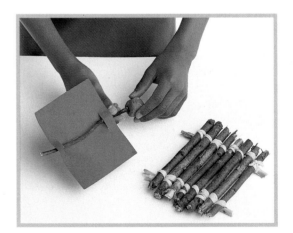

1 Cut out a square of paper for the sail. Cut two slits in the paper, as shown, and thread a stick through them. Glue a paper sun on to the sail.

2 Put eight sticks of the same length next to each other and lay a stick across each end. Tie the sticks tightly together with pieces of raffia.

3 Push one end of the stick mast into a lump of modelling clay. Then push the modelling clay firmly in place on the middle of the raft.

Making the catamaran

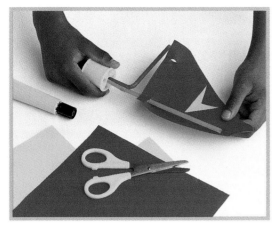

1 Cut out a triangle of paper for the sail and make a slit in each corner. Push two straws into a cotton reel and thread them on to the sail, as shown.

2 Paint three lollipop sticks and let them dry. Then glue them across two cotton reels. Glue the cotton reel and sail to the middle of the sticks.

3 Glue the flat ends of the corks on to the ends of the cotton reels. Then, make a flag with the bent end of a straw and push it on to the mast.

Setting sail

Place the boats gently on the water and see how they float. The catamaran will float best if the mast is stuck right in the centre of the lollipop sticks. Turn the boats until the sails catch the wind and see which one goes fastest!

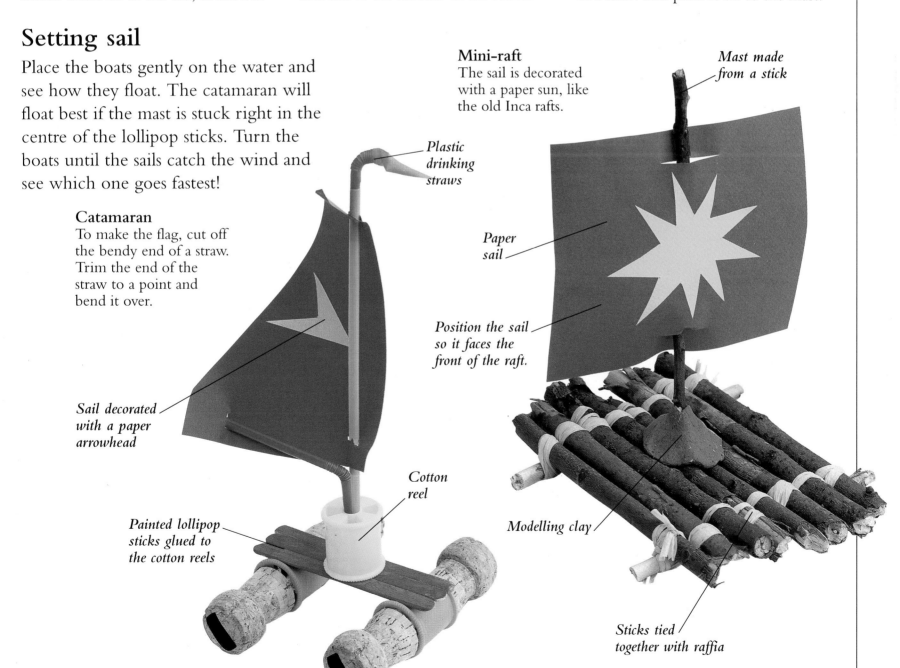

Mini-raft
The sail is decorated with a paper sun, like the old Inca rafts.

Mast made from a stick

Plastic drinking straws

Paper sail

Catamaran
To make the flag, cut off the bendy end of a straw. Trim the end of the straw to a point and bend it over.

Position the sail so it faces the front of the raft.

Sail decorated with a paper arrowhead

Cotton reel

Painted lollipop sticks glued to the cotton reels

Modelling clay

Sticks tied together with raffia

NATURE'S MODELS

On a quiet afternoon, why not try making a model with some of the things you have collected outdoors? With a little imagination you can transform twigs, fir cones, leaves, and feathers into works of art. Here and overleaf you can find out how to create tiny mice, a corn dolly, a wooden seagull, and a sunflower.

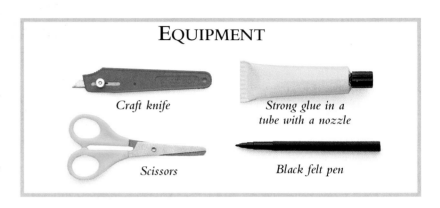

EQUIPMENT

Craft knife

Strong glue in a tube with a nozzle

Scissors

Black felt pen

You will need

For the corn dolly

For the sunflower

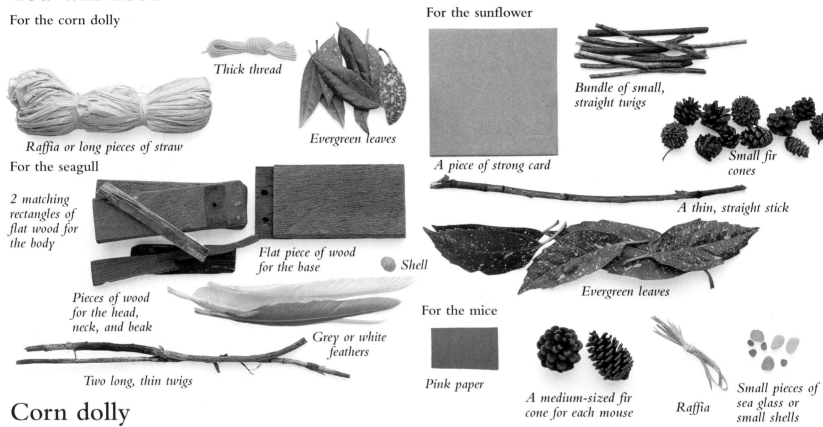

Thick thread

Evergreen leaves

Raffia or long pieces of straw

Bundle of small, straight twigs

A piece of strong card

Small fir cones

For the seagull

2 matching rectangles of flat wood for the body

Flat piece of wood for the base

Shell

A thin, straight stick

Pieces of wood for the head, neck, and beak

Grey or white feathers

Evergreen leaves

For the mice

Two long, thin twigs

Pink paper

A medium-sized fir cone for each mouse

Raffia

Small pieces of sea glass or small shells

Corn dolly

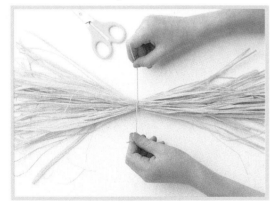

1 Cut 25 or so pieces of raffia about 25 cm long. Tie them together in the middle with thick thread to make the doll's waist.

2 Divide the raffia in half below the waist to make two legs. Tie thread round each leg at the top, in the middle, and near the bottom.

3 Tie thread round the doll's chest, and split the raffia above it into three sections. Tie the two outer sections, as shown, to make arms.

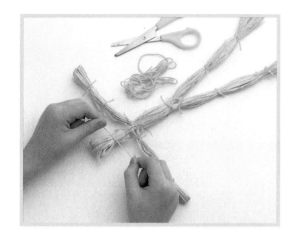

4 Tie thread round the raffia just above the arms to make a neck. Then fold back the raffia and tie it at the neck, as shown, to make the head.

5 Wind pieces of raffia round the doll's body and neck to make them look fatter, then tie the ends and tuck them into the doll's body.

6 Make a dress by tying leaves to the doll's waist with a piece of raffia. Make a hat out of small leaves and attach it to her head.

Seagull sculpture

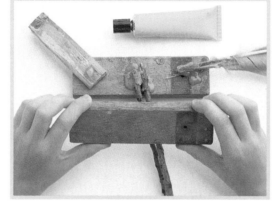

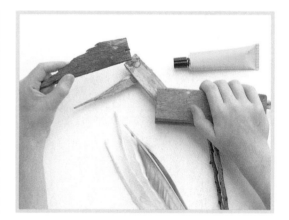

1 Glue two twigs to one of the matching rectangles of wood for legs. Glue on two tail feathers, then add a small piece of wood for a neck.

2 Glue the other matching wooden rectangle in place over the first, to cover the places where the legs, neck, and tail feathers join the body.

3 Glue a thin piece of wood to the back of the neck for the lower beak. Glue a larger piece of wood to the front of the neck for the head.

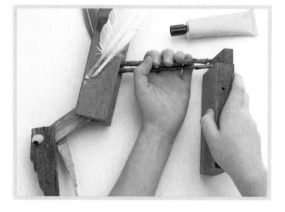

4 Glue two feathers to each side of the bird's body for wings, so that the back set of feathers points upwards and the front set points downwards.

5 Glue a small shell to the bird's head to make an eye. Draw a small black circle on the shell to look like the pupil of the eye.

6 Let the glue dry hard, then glue the bird's legs into a flat piece of wood, to make a stand. (Ask an adult to make two holes in the wood for you.)

NATURE GALLERY

Sunflower on a stick

1 Cut a circle out of a thick piece of card. Glue small fir cones over the circle to make the centre of the flower. Leave the glue to dry.

2 Turn the circle of card over. Glue short, straight twigs with large leaves between them to the back of the circle to form the petals.

3 Glue a long, straight stick to the bottom of the card circle. Let the glue dry and set completely before turning the sunflower over.

On display

The models you make will vary depending on the materials you have to hand, but that just makes them more interesting. Use the models here as starting points for your own ideas.

Corn dolly

You can dress your corn dolly with any natural materials you can find. Look for things like seedheads, twigs, bark, and dried flowers.

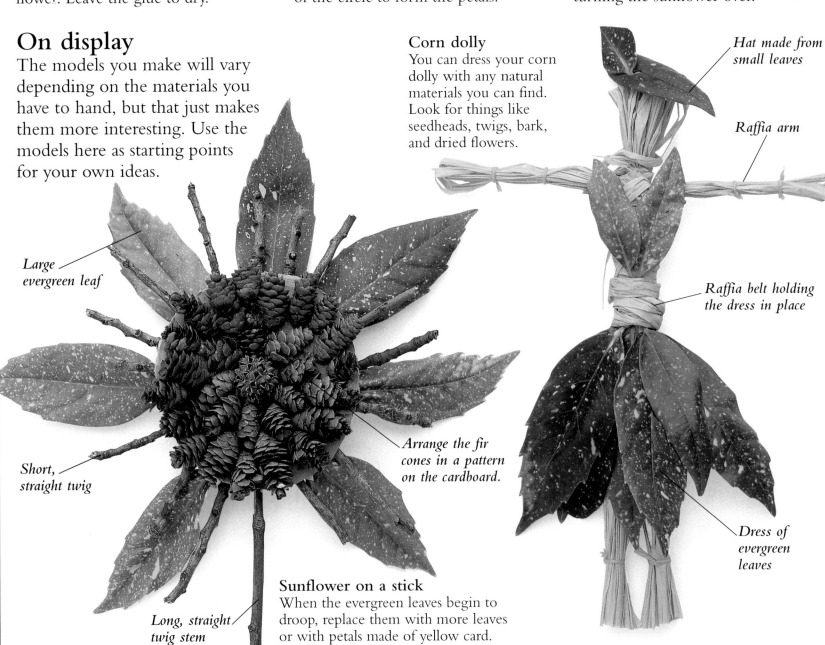

Large evergreen leaf

Short, straight twig

Arrange the fir cones in a pattern on the cardboard.

Long, straight twig stem

Sunflower on a stick
When the evergreen leaves begin to droop, replace them with more leaves or with petals made of yellow card.

Hat made from small leaves

Raffia arm

Raffia belt holding the dress in place

Dress of evergreen leaves

Fir cone mice

1 Glue two small pieces of sea glass or shells to the front of the cone under the open end. These are feet for the cones to balance on.

2 Cut two small ears out of pink paper and fold them in the middle. Glue them in place near the top of the fir cone for ears.

3 Glue on two tiny pieces of sea glass for eyes below the ears. Cut short pieces of raffia for the tail and whiskers, and glue them in place.

Triangular piece of wood for the head

Eye made from a shell painted with a black circle

Fir cone mice
Why not make several little mice and stand them together to look as if they are playing?

Narrow triangle of wood for the beak

Raffia tail

Pink card ears

Seagull sculpture
This seagull is made from leftover scraps of wood, but driftwood would work well too. Look for pieces that make you think of a head or beak. Then why not try to make some other birds and animals?

Rectangles of wood for the body

Legs made from long twigs

Wings and tail made from real seagull feathers

Small fir cone for the body

Strong, flat piece of wood for a stand

Raffia whiskers

Sea glass eyes

Tiny feet made from pieces of sea glass

61

HANDY HINTS

This picture guide illustrates skills you will find helpful with some of the projects in this book. If you want to practise your reef knots, use different coloured rope or string as in the steps below.

Using a compass

1 Hold the compass steady in your hand and away from anything metal. Then wait until the coloured end of the needle stops moving.

2 Turn the compass around until the coloured end of the needle lines up with the symbol for North. You are now facing magnetic North.

Hammering in a nail

1 Using a ruler and pencil, make marks on the exact positions where you want the nails to go into the piece of wood.

2 Hold the nail about half way down and place it on a pencil mark. Give it a firm tap with the hammer to drive it into the wood.

3 Remove your hand and, holding the hammer near the end, hit the nail squarely until its head lies on the surface of the wood.

Tying a reef knot

1 Hold the ends of two pieces of rope or string in each hand. Wrap the end of the green rope over then under the end of the yellow rope.

2 Now take the free end of the green rope and place it right over and then across the end of the yellow rope.

3 Finally, wrap the green rope right around the yellow rope and up through the hole in the middle, then pull both ends of rope tightly.

OUTDOOR CODE

Whatever you are doing outside, whether just going for a walk, or arranging a nature expedition, plan your activities sensibly and take care of the countryside and its wildlife. Here are some important points to remember.

•

Always tell your parents or carers where you are going and what you plan to do.

•

Before setting off, make sure you are wearing suitable clothes, have any equipment or food you need, and change for a phone call home.

•

Do not drop litter. Take any rubbish home with you.

•

Keep to paths and fasten all gates behind you.

•

Always leave things as you found them. Do not damage any plants or trees.

•

When collecting things in the wild, only take what you need and make sure you leave plenty of specimens behind.

•

Only pick wild flowers if there are plenty growing, and just pick a few. Never pick rare plants or uproot any plant.

•

Never disturb nesting birds or take birds' eggs.

•

Be gentle with any creatures you catch. Study them gently, and make notes quickly, then put them back where you found them.

INDEX

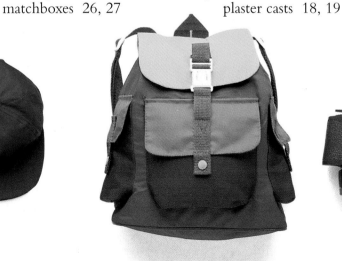